Thank you for engaging the WORL&D while picking my bro

Engage the WORL&D!

A WHIMSICAL, BRAIN-PICKING "MEME-OIR" FROM A CREATIVE DIGITAL LEARNING STRATEGIST

Zsolt Olah

VIZIPOKE
PRESS

Philadelphia, PA

Zsolt Olah
Vizipoke Press
5 Hastings Ave
Havertown, PA 19083
www.vizipoke.com

Ordering Information:
Quantity sales. Special discounts are available on quantity purchases by corporations, associations, and others. For details, contact the "Special Sales Department" at the address above.

Engage the WORL&D! / Zsolt Olah. -- 1st ed.
ISBN 978-0-9996823-0-2

To Sophie, Imi, Leslie, and Lemon.

"Is this page intentionally left blank?"
— Tom

Contents

Acknowledgments

My Kids

The day our son was admitted to the intensive-care unit, he had just turned three. Sophie, his twin sister, called us from their room at 9 p.m. to say "Imi isn't feeling well." He was not. Imi and Sophie were about to start a new day care the next day. My wife and I spent the night in the intensive care with Imi. The next day, with Grandpa, Sophie went to a new school, and stayed there for the whole day, on her own. The bravest thing a three-year-old can do. She only had one question. She knew the rule was one stuffed animal per person. She would have liked to take both Doggy and Nemo, so she wouldn't hurt their feelings. Meanwhile, Imi spent three weeks on a life-support machine in the intensive care.

Both our kids are teenagers now. In fifteen years, they have taught me a lot about life, values, and perspectives. I'm looking forward to learning a lot more from them in the years to come.

My Wife

In the year 2000 I wrote my first screenplay. I forced my wife to read the whole thing. We're still married. Thanks for the support on this endeavor, and for my birthday present: vouchers to take care of everything while I write this book.

My Family

I also want to thank my parents, who not only contributed to the book itself, but throughout my life have supported me in constantly pushing the envelope. My sister, who loves reading books, and my grandparents who used to read me books.

Colleagues

Professionally, I owe everyone who trusted me with their investment on the Kickstarter campaign, and then pestered me online to make this happen. I didn't know what to expect when I started a Kickstarter campaign, and I am humbled by each of the thirty people who trusted me not screwing this up:

Thank you so much for your support:

Anthony Reisinger
Beata Olah-Wood
Bill Ryan
Bobbi Block
Brian Binder
Chris Coladonato
Connie Malamed
David Anderson
Dr. Olah Janos
Jeff Spoelker
Karl M. Kapp
Karthik Chidambaram
Kristy Blaise
Lucas Blair
Maria Cipollone
Matt Guyan
Matthew Bibby
Megan Torrance
Michelle
Odeh Muhawesh
Seth Grandeau
Shannon Tipton
Tracy Carroll
Troy Stein
Zynthi Martinez

You

I want to thank YOU. I don't know who you are, where you are, or what you do. I don't know what made you read this book. But if you learn anything useful, or just enjoy the ride; I want to know who you are, where you are, and what you do! Let's connect! Let's engage the WORL&D!

And thanks Lisa for not freaking out when editing the book! Your comments and suggestions were greatly appreciated. (I did break some of your rules, though.)

Thanks for reading this!
Zsolt (@rabbitoreg)

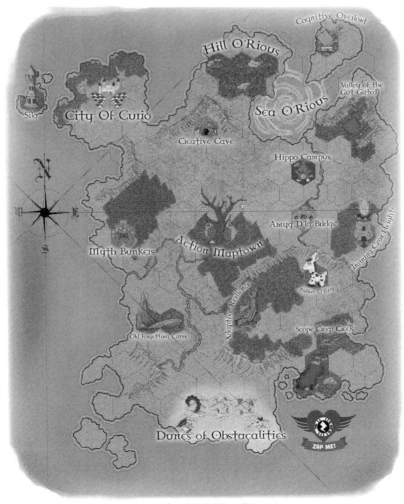

The WORL&D

(To learn more about the WORL&D, download the Zappar augmented reality app, and scan this picture!)

Chapter Zero

CALL TO ADVENTURE

"No, no! The adventures first, explanations take such a dreadful time." — Lewis Carroll

You're about to pick my brain to see the WORL&D from my perspective. My "meme-oir" is a mental tapas–style entree, with freshly dug ingredients such as memories turned a-ha moments harvested in the field of learning and development, topped with a pinch of whimsicality spice, a dash of humor, and sprinkles of memes. Served chilled for anyone in L&D, specifically garnished for instructional designers. Pair it with your favorite glass of beverage, relax, don't forget to breathe, and prepare to engage the WORL&D!

Are you the kind of serious person who leaves pages intentionally blank? This memeoir is not for you, then. Are you looking for some quick templates with step-by-step instructions on how to create training? There are much better resources for that. Are you interested in the in-depth knowledge of a buzzword method that makes learning magically happen? Check out the fairy tales section in your local library.

As Donald Taylor, chair of the Learning and Performance Institute, says in his blog:

"Learning is like breathing: superficially understood yet fundamentally complex and essential to life."

I'm not you. I don't have your mind, I don't know your circumstances.

I can't promise, even if you were to follow my path, that you would end up at the same place. You control your own breathing! The most I can do is to show relevance, challenge your thinking to engage your mind, maybe even motivate you to change your breathing. Laughter is one way to do that.

If you've ever wanted to "pick someone's creative brain," you're onto something here. Expect a gameful, borderline whimsical, often Hill O'Rious storytelling memoir of a Sea O'Rious topic: staying relevant in the corporate learning and development (L&D) field through six traits of instructional design. When I say storytelling, I mean lots of mental travel in space and time to distant destinations of relevant a-ha moments of learning. Some will take your breath away, some will make you gasp, some will make you laugh, some might even make you yawn. Either case, expect some breathing challenges along the way!

What's a mental travel anyway?

MENTAL TRAVEL: Hungary, 1970s
(Where an open-loop trauma happens.)

It is the roaring seventies. We're behind the Iron Curtain in the so-called Eastern Bloc. I remember falling asleep to Lewis Carroll's *Through the Looking-Glass* every night (granted, it is dubbed in Hungarian, my native language). Carroll's book is a chess-inspired dream-story of a Pawn getting promoted to Queen. I still remember the crackling sound of the vinyl player, bringing this wonderfully weirdo world of *Through the Looking-Glass* alive. I do root for Alice. I want her to beat all the odds. She's a little lost and lonely, like pages intentionally left blank. I want her to get promoted. Except, by the time we reach the end of side one of the vinyl, I am usually asleep or too zoned out to flip it. And so, most of the time, Alice won't get promoted to Queen. The unfinished story creates an open loop in my brain. According to the Zeigarnik effect, the brain does not like unfinished actions and open loops! Therefore, this childhood open-loop trauma still haunts me today. I feel like a gompie, living next door to Alice for the last twenty-four years. Nobody wants to feel like a gompie! The loop must be closed! Here and now.

This book is an attempt to close a chapter, and the open loop in my life. The idea of the book comes from a challenge by Shannon Tipton, author and Chief Learning Rebel. Shannon challenged me to write a blog for thirty days, every single day. My daily stories were self-reflections on learning via a-ha moments. After completing the thirty-day challenge, my blog entries revealed an uncanny resemblance between the world of L&D today and Alice's situation in *Through the Looking-Glass*.

So, Who the [Bleep] Is Alice?

"Alice is in her room, alone. Her parents don't really involve her in adult conversations. She does have a cat to play with, but other than that, Alice is not really social. She's literally living in her silo room. Alice would love to play chess. In fact, she's good at chess if people would give her a chance to prove it. It's just that she has nobody to play with; she doesn't have a seat at the adults' table. As she's standing in front of the looking glass, reflecting, she knows she has a decision to make: should she stay or should she go? And then, curiosity drives her to step through, into a new, magical world— a little upside down, a little nonsensical. Alice knows that the world around her has changed, and she needs to find and prove herself again. She must beat the Red King. It's a journey of transitioning from Pawn to Queen, where, at the end, she would have a seat at the table. Don't get me wrong; she's not so bleeping innocent. She does have an attitude. But she's curious and willing to do whatever it takes to finish that journey. Throughout her learning journey, often clinging to her old-world beliefs, Alice faces lots of obstacles and strange figures. At the end of the day, she needs to unlearn, relearn, and adapt to a new world to succeed. Welcome to *Through the Looking Glass (and the World Alice Found There)*!"

Now, imagine the same story from the L&D perspective.

Who the [Bleep] Is L&D?

"L&D is in her room, alone. The business doesn't really involve her in adult conversations. She does have an LMS to play with, but other than that, L&D is not really social. She's literally living in her silo room. L&D would love to make a difference. In fact, she's good at making a difference if people would give her a chance to prove it. It's just that she has nobody to work with; she doesn't have a seat at the business table. As she's standing in front of the looking class, reflecting, she knows she has a decision to make: should she stay or should she go? And then, curiosity drives her to step through into a new, magical WORL&D—a little upside down, a little nonsensical. L&D knows that the WORL&D around her has changed, and she needs to find and prove herself again. She must beat the Red King. It's a journey of transitioning from order-taker to problem-solver, where, at the end, she would have a seat at the table. Don't get me wrong; she's not so bleeping innocent. She does have an attitude. But she's curious and willing to do whatever it takes to finish that journey. Throughout her learning journey, often clinging to her old-world beliefs, L&D faces lots of obstacalities and strange stakeholders. At the end of the day, she needs to unlearn, relearn, and adapt to a new WORL&D to succeed. Welcome to *Through the Looking Class (and the WORL&D L&D Found There)!*"

Is Storytelling Gameful?

I love to think of storytelling as an adventure game. The adventure comes alive through human interactions between a storyteller and their audience. As with any game, there are rules in place to make the gameplay fun and engaging. Storytelling is not simply telling facts or presenting data. When designed and played well, a well-crafted story gets your audience hooked. Literally. In "Why Your Brain Loves Good Storytelling," Paul J. Zak shows how his lab confirmed the drug, oxytocin, released in the blood after watching a "good story."[1] Oxytocin is the drug of trust; it tells our brain to connect, to help and be nice to each other. This is a drug that reassures we're in a safe place.

This book is about my successes and failures as a lifelong learner in the pursuit of staying relevant in the field of L&D. It is not a "how to" resource on how to become a better learning professional (there are plenty of those books already). Many of the stories you'll hear are "whimsical," which is a word often used to describe my work. I'll do my best to stay serious, but what can you expect from a "hoot" (the other word I often get)? But no good game or story ever starts with learning objectives. The best games and stories start with adventures, dreadful explanations come later. Let's hear about the adventure!

---

1   https://hbr.org/2014/10/why-your-brain-loves-good-storytelling.

Where Does the Adventure Take Place?

I learned public speaking from Perry Mason, math from Lewis Carroll, psychology from Agatha Christie, self-help from Edgar Allan Poe, critical thinking from Douglas Adams, but one my most memorable teachers was the grandmaster of storytelling, Gabriel Garcia Marquez. When I moved to the United States, I brought with me two dictionaries (a.k.a. "static Google") and a copy of his signature book, *One Hundred Years of Solitude*. After twenty-four years in L&D (feels more like a hundred), I have to confess: I've never read the foreword of a book, I've never watched the preview of a movie. I'm all for the adventure, where the real story begins. The adventure starts here and now. But like every story, we need a hero, and I pick YOU.

You're Not a Hero?

Just as Alice needs to unlearn prior knowledge, skills, behaviors, and practice critical thinking to change her own beliefs while navigating the new world, L&D is facing similar challenges today. Unlearning is hard. It can be frustrating and painful. It's hard because unlearning is not simply forgetting; it's changing your own beliefs. It's the first necessary step before you can break a habit, and build new ones. Good news is, it's all in your head. Bad news is, it's all in your head. What makes someone a hero is stepping out of the comfort zone into this uncomfortable, unknown place with an open mind. If you're willing to do that, you're a hero.

What Does a Hero Do?

A hero asks good questions. One thing you'll notice along this adventure is we're asking a lot of questions. In fact, the most important advice I can give to those just entering the WORL&D is simply this: before you jump into finding answers to questions, make sure the right questions were asked! And one of the most important questions you might ask yourself is: *Am I asking the right questions?*

A hero acts, while others talk. Ready to jump in? Buckle up, we're going on a trip! A mental trip is the recollection of an event from memory, kind of like a "that reminds me" visit down memory lane. It's a travel in space and time in memory. Memory recall is a process of reimagination of past events. Unlike a movie recorded on your DVR that you can rewatch any time, the memory recall process is more like getting the actors together to shoot the movie again, based on how much you remember of the script. It's like starting from scratch every time. Therefore, my memories (and yours) are subject to change. Events taking place since the memory was encoded can, and will, affect my recollections. Why is it important to remember this? Because my mental travels can be dangerous and unreliable! Proceed with caution!

MENTAL TRAVEL: Hungary, 1980
(When curiosity killed the train.)

It is on the floor of our living room, at the tender age of nine, when I realize the meaning of the old saying "curiosity killed the train." What I'm curious about is the speed of my toy train. The train travels pretty slowly when powered by the proper 9V battery. *Would it go much faster if I plugged it in into the 220V?* (Remember, this is Europe. We have 220 voltage.) In case you're curious too, the answer is no. The train won't go faster. It won't go anywhere at all. As I plug the wire into the socket on the wall, the question is answered by a big loud bang. Smoke and darkness ensue as the main fuse is blown in the house. Little do I know that blowing up trains will be my life in the future (as in pushing the envelope when it comes to training—pun intended … you're welcome).

You don't get sore muscles by watching *The Biggest Loser.* You get them by doing exercises. People learn by making mistakes—even better, by reflecting on their mistakes. Curious people learn by blowing up train(ing)s. Why? Because curiosity is the fuel driving creativity, innovation, and other people nuts by constantly asking the same questions: Why? What if?

What if? What if the Last ID On Earth decided to step into the unknown, through the looking class, to unlearn, adjust, and adapt to the new WORL&D? What if there was a giant conspiracy after our hero, led by the Red King and his infamous Scythe? What if our hero was going through a mental travel with me through space and time to reflect on six missing memory traits of the Magic Mojo Hexad, the only hope against the Red King?

Never heard of the Magic Mojo Hexad? The Magic Mojo Hexad is an ancient L&D shield with six powerful traits:

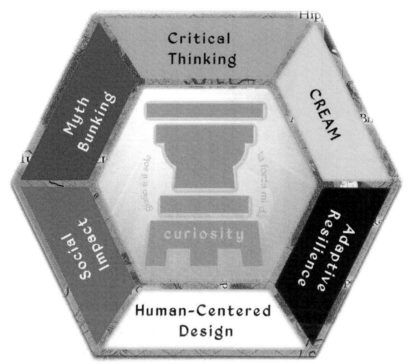

Magic Mojo Hexad Shield

Nobody knows what skills you will need five or ten years from now. However, these six traits with the underlying curiosity engine will provide you with a solid foundation. You will need all six missing traits of the Magic Mojo Hexad to face the ultimate enemy, the Red King, and his dreaded Scythe. And so, a hero is born today.

#WhoIsLiDoe?

In this gameful adventure book, you will witness the transformation of the **Last ID On E**arth (LI DOE).

LI DOE (Last ID On Earth)

As LI DOE enters the whimsical WORL&D of *Through the Looking Class,* his mission is to break the Red King's spell (business goal). To do that, LI DOE must escape the SILO, and lead the L&D folks to the light by getting promoted to Queen (performance objectives). To get promoted, LI DOE must unlearn, relearn, and adapt (learning objectives). You will notice we refer to LI DOE both as she and he. That is not a mistake. In the WORL&D, gender doesn't matter. What matters is the ability of the underlying Artificial Intelligence (AI) framework that powers LI DOE and her decisions. And guess what? LI DOE will rely on you to improve his AI engine. I'll guide LI DOE through the travels in my time and my space, exploring my reflections on learning, but it's not me. It's you—the reader—who must collect and encode those reflections; it's you who can turn your own a-ha moments into lessons learned to beat the Red King in real life (IRL). Your real-life actions will determine whether LI DOE can succeed in the WORL&D. You'll have to find the same missing traits in real life as LI DOE is pursuing in the imaginary WORL&D.

What are the six missing traits of Magic Mojo Hexad?

1. **Critical Thinking** (From Order-taking to Problem-solving by Critical Thinking)

2. **CREAM** (From Page-turning to Mind-blowing by CReativity, Engagement, And Motivation)

3. **Adaptive Resilience** (From Passive Resistance to Adaptive Resilience by The Art of Bouncing Back)

4. **Human-Centered Design** (From Content to Context by Design and Game Thinking)

5. **Social Impact** (From Silo to Sharing by Work-out-loud, Personal-brand, and Relationships)

6. **Myth Bunking** (From Learning Myths to the Real Workplace Thing by The Science of Learning, Artificial Intelligence, Evidence-Based Practicality, Knowledge-Skills-Attitude)

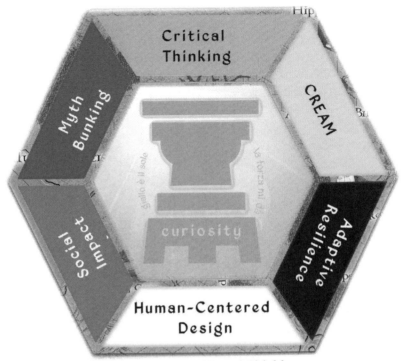

Magic Mojo Hexad Shield

We'll explore these traits one by one in the book through stories. Storytelling, especially if you're working in L&D, is a fundamental skill. Have you been to a seminar, presentation, or conference where all you can remember is the story the presenter told at the start? Did you notice how speeches generally start out with a personal story? That's not a coincidence. So, let's hop on the ride! Is it going to be safe the entire ride? Probably not. We're going to visit the Iron Curtain, bring down a Communist regime, blow up the dot-com era, survive corporate training at a time when "game" is considered a four-letter word, explore the world of artificial neural networks, unlearn a slough of learning myths, and reflect.

Am I Asking the Right Questions?

At this point, one of the right questions you might ask is: what's so gameful about reading this memeoir? Learning from a book is great, but it will never replace doing the thing. While I'm guiding you through this adventure on paper, after each chapter I'm going to ask you to go undercover in your own real WORL&D! Wherever you are, whatever you do, just keep doing it! Imagine today you stepped through the looking class, and you are now in your WORL&D. You must not only survive but thrive! You will look at things from LI DOE's perspective. I'm going to ask you to complete critical missions without blowing your cover. You think the Red King is not real? Do not ever underestimate the power of the Red King! He's probably already in your head. Did you hear a voice saying, *It's silly to have a page with "Is this page intentionally left blank?" on it?* There he is. Do you ever hear voices criticizing you, telling you something won't work? Raising doubt? Urging you to postpone? Asking you to reconsider? Ridiculing you before that important presentation? That's the Red King. Do you occasionally forget the names of things and notions? Even worse, have you ever gone to the basement only to realize you forgot why? There it is. The Red King.

You are powering AI behind the Last ID On Earth, the only hero to stop the Red King and lead the L&D folks to the light! A new generation of instructional designers are looking to be challenged, engaged, motivated, and inspired by your actions. You are a hero! Your superpower is in the value you create in people's mind, not what content you plug into course templates. Therefore, the value you bring is often invisible; many times nobody will know it was you who brought it. If you want a career with shiny badges and constant spotlights, now is a good time to run far away from L&D.

So, Do You Accept the Challenge with LI DOE?

If you're not sure, that's completely fine: put the book down and come back later!

If you're ready to take on the challenge: let's shake the gates of boredom! Let's Engage the WORL&D! Bring it on, Red King!

Fine Print: *This adventure may or may not cause side effects, including but not limited to: critical thinking, engagement in the science of learning, motivation in doing, exploration of storytelling, and other game mechanics. Stories from the life of the unreliable narrator may cause rhythmic, vocalized, expiatory, and involuntary actions, also known as laughter. Laughter lasting more than four hours may cause frictions in your social relationships. By the end of this adventure, some participants may be inspired to learn more. Inspiration is normal, and can be controlled by resources at the end of the book. Assuming the identity of LI DOE is not an identity theft. Some who went through the adventure reported higher levels of adrenalin while working undercover. Adrenalin is not for everyone. Ask your L&D professional if engagement is right for you! Engage the WORL&D!*

As I said, I never read forewords. But I surely hope you read my introduction, titled "Chapter Zero" in an attempt to lure you in.

IN REAL LIFE (IRL) CHALLENGES:

At the end of each chapter, you'll find some IRL challenges. If you just want to read the book, you may skip them. If you're competitive, complete the challenges before moving on. And if you're super-competitive, check out **Engage the WORL&D!** challenge cards on http://www.engagetheworldbook.com!

In real life, assess yourself on a 1 (no experience) to 10 (expert) scale on the six traits of the Magic Mojo Hexad. Add the six numbers together. This is your mojo power to start with:

1. **Critical Thinking** (From Order-taking to Problem-solving by Critical Thinking)
2. **CREAM** (From Page-turning to Mind-blowing by CReativity, Engagement, And Motivation)
3. **Adaptive Resilience** (From Passive Resistance to Adaptive Resilience by The Art of Bouncing Back)
4. **Human-Centered Design** (From Content to Context by Design and Game Thinking)
5. **Social Impact** (From Silo to Sharing by Work-out-loud, Personal-brand, and Relationships)
6. **Myth Bunking** (From Learning Myths to the Real Workplace Thing by The Science of Learning, Artificial Intelligence, Evidence-Based Practicality, Knowledge-Skills-Attitude)

Chapter One

THE CURIOUS MIND
(FROM REALITY TO THE WORL&D)

Welcome to the mental trip beyond the looking class! Every journey, even mental ones, needs a map. My memories, just like everyone else's, are unreliable. Therefore, this mental map should give a good glimpse of where we're heading.

This is *Through the Looking Class (and the WORL&D LI DOE found there)*.

Where Are We?

The City of Curio, in the North-East corner, is one of the most peculiar places in the WORL&D. Everything in the city is labeled: the ancient streets, buildings, lamps, trees, even randomly roaming chickens. The labels are color-coded to make it easier to categorize objects. What makes this place stand out in the WORL&D is that nobody lives here anymore. If you're curious, you're in the right place. The City of Curio was built during the Great Virus by L&D folks forgotten ever since. People are forgotten. But not the SILO, the source of wonder in the WORL&D, left behind on a nearby island.

You might describe the SILO as a rook-like structure with five doors at the bottom. Legend has it that a magical disease hit the WORL&D once, after all copies of Gabriel Garcia Marquez's *One Hundred Years of Solitude* were stolen from the library. The plague spread like wildfire. (*One Hundred Years of Solitude* is about the City of Mirrors, where residents, among other things, get hit by a strange plague. As a result, they're forgetting words and meanings. In order to preserve their memories, they start labeling everything—from forks and houses to chairs and cows—just to remind themselves what things are called.)

What happened in *One Hundred Years of Solitude* is exactly what is going on in the WORL&D. Residents are forgetting memorized facts, seemingly useless dates of events, terms and definitions, blooming action verbs, even the foundations of L&D, which distinguished this world when its founding brothers, Hill and Sea O'Rious, first settled here.

The Origins of the WORL&D

According to legend, the ships of the O'Rious brothers were driven by curiosity, the never-ending combustion fuel of creativity and innovation, as they sailed through seven seas and nine Gagne events. The long trip took its toll on Sea and Hill O'Rious. After a nasty adult learning theory fight, they decided to still work together in some whimsical ways, but to live separate microlearning lives. Sea owned the water around the island, while Hill ruled the land. They learned happily ever after, generation upon generation.

While Hill and Sea O'Rious predicted the coming virus, they had no cure for it. To combat the virus, residents designed an elaborate machine that would save everyone's L&D memories for generations to come. They called it the SOLITUDE, named after the book itself. Folks used the ADDIE model to complete this super-complex learning machine. Unfortunately, people's memories working on the analysis, design, and development waterfall process deteriorated dramatically, so new people had to pick up the slack. Residents got to the point where nobody really remembered the analysis, much less why they were building this thing in the first place.

One fact they did manage to remember, however, was its name: SILOTUDE (which was itself already a false memory). Even worse, when the resident tasked with painting the word "SILOTUDE" on the building took a short bio break halfway through, the unthinkable happened. By the time he returned to work on the long corporate ladder, he was staring at the word "SILO." He vaguely remembered there was supposed to be more to it, but he couldn't recall what it was. Therefore, it was unthinkable. This is a typical difference between knowing and recalling (this little-known fact didn't help out our friend, nor move my story forward). And so, the label just stayed as is: SILO. Evaluation, of course, never took place. The SILO was forgotten for centuries to come.

Until one day, under the ruling of the self-proclaimed Red King, a group of serious eLearning L&D folks looking for a hiding place in the library basement found an old copy of *One Hundred Years of Solitude*. And there it was: a storyboard for the SILO and the origins of the WORL&D[2]

That's when they learned about the SILO and an upcoming threat to the WORL&D in the shape of an evil person named Captain Saicin. Unfortunately, nobody recognized Captain Saicin until it was too late. Today he is known as the Red King. They also learned that one day a hero arrives, a hero who's going to lead the L&D folks to the light and beat the Red King. And that hero will appear in the SILO. The L&D folks then took shelter inside the SILO, waiting for the hero's arrival.

Miraculously, the SILO has been working ever since it was created. And by working, I mean there's stranger things going on inside.

What's Going On Inside the SILO?

While the outside of the SILO is totally unremarkable, inside is one of the most complex contraptions in the WORL&D. Today, we just started discovering its basic functions. Some WORL&D scientists say we're still scratching the surface.

---

2   See video clip: https://www.youtube.com/watch?v=qTaaDLeSR6o

So, what's inside the SILO? Well, there's LI DOE, of course, who has no idea how she got here in the first place! Actually, this is very important. It's all about the mindset here! In the WORL&D, you don't step in or go to anywhere. Really!! You can't physically go anywhere, unless your mind is already there. Everything in the WORL&D starts with your mindset. While this may sound strange at first, once you get the hang of it, you can go anywhere with ease. On the other hand, if you don't control your thinking, your body may feel like a gray gompie in the fog, lost and lonely at random times.

LI DOE finds himself in a dark elevator, going down. He lifts up his foot to spot his future-gazing mixed-reality goggles cracked.
LI DOE: "Oops."

He puts them back anyway. The elevator door opens to reveal the lobby. LI DOE tries to exit but his muscles are not moving. Let's focus on the lobby while he's trying! The SILO has five entrances. Each door is labeled: SIGHT, SOUND, TOUCH, SMELL, and TASTE. Rumor has it there's a sixth door, but again, unfortunately, they didn't get to document its functionality due to creep scope. Overall, the business goal for the SILO was to cure the "forgetting disease."

Legend says it took generations for the WORL&D to build the right training to eliminate forgetting. On paper, it did. In reality, it's not cured yet totally; it's just curbed. Dr. Ebbenhaus, a local mathematician, invented a formula that somewhat curbed the total effect. Since formulas aren't marketable, they replaced it with a curve. They labeled it the "forgetting curve." There's a monument today in the South of the WORL&D, commemorating the event.

You can't spend too much time at the monument, for memory security reasons. Best way to visit the place is to pace your tour over time. Tourist guides call this "microtouring." Short, bite-size chunks of visits with time breaks in-between.

Ever since the rediscovery of the SILO, researchers have been trying to figure out its complex structure and mechanism. Turns out, while researchers agree on the generic structure, it is clear that it will take many more generations to come to crack the code inside. They just recently discovered the shady underground part of the SILO. The WORL&D is eager to learn more about this wonder, as it affects the most valuable asset of the island: the human mind.

Speaking of humans. LI DOE suddenly found herself inside a classroom, locked in with a handful of L&D folks. They're sitting on imaginary chairs, with their hands behind the back. Their expression is frozen in time, as they stare at a sketch of Scythe on the blackboard. LI DOE's machine-learning algorithm finds patterns and analyzes data in a wink, but LI DOE has no idea what to do with this picture. This doesn't match any learning patterns.

A couple of pages later, you will not remember most of this story. That's all right. Forgetting is part of learning. In fact, a very important part of learning.

Nanu Nanu! Do You Remember?

As LI DOE's mind wonders about the Scythe, he finds himself teleported into a waiting room. Remember, your thoughts (or the lack of) determine your moves in the WORL&D. Where the mind goes, the body follows. LI DOE can clearly see the restricted area in front, called Sensory Memory. The five entrance doors in the Sensory Memory open and shut constantly in milliseconds. Each door has a filter allowing only a certain type of reflection of the outside WORL&D: vision, sound, touch, smell, and taste. Reflections don't live long here. It's a messy process. Fortunately, most of these dull reflections do not make it to the waiting area where LI DOE stands. Most reflections fall into a sinkhole in seconds. They disappear like a gray gompie in the fog.

LI DOE focuses on a reflection that teleports him to a larger waiting area, labeled SHORT-TERM MEMORY. The room has about seven seats. Right now, two of them are occupied already from a previous recall. From time to time, the loudspeaker blares: "Attention!" calling a reflection's ID number. The reflection item then moves on toward the LTM (long-term memory) section. If an item is not called for a while, it ends up in a sinkhole.

Reflections transferred to the LTM go through an internal process, called "Encoding." The walls of the long corridor swing open to release millions of star-looking bright spots (they call them neurons here). The whole encoding process is a cacophony of smell, noise, images, videos, texture, and who knows what. LI DOE's collecting SILO data. The bigger the data inside his artificial neural network, the better decision-maker he becomes. It's a lifelong learning process. And while LI DOE doesn't know this, her AI features are still there, but many of them got reset while going through the looking class. Therefore, LI DOE must unlearn and relearn a lot, before he can use them effectively.

The data mining suddenly teleports LI DOE to a much calmer area of the SILO: the Recall Department. The Recall Department is like a movie multiplex with hundreds of 3-D theaters. As LI DOE enters one, she sees no seats, only a giant mirror. The door shuts behind and the lights go off. LI DOE can't even catch himself in the mirror. Stranger things start happening. In the complete darkness and silence, LI DOE can literally hear her own mind churning the algorithm to make sense of this whole experience. At least, that's what LI DOE thinks. But let's not forget, it's my mind! Remember, this mental travel is all about my memories. Or better to say, my meme-ories. For no reason at all, I think of the word "grandma."

3-D holograms flash in the dark: a vision of a grandma. Food. Taste. The texture of old clothes. Books she used to read. Old home. Mudbricks. Pancakes. Smoke. We're flooded with memories. A wolf.

A wolf? Why in the WORL&D a wolf? Remember, we're traveling in my WORL&D, along with my memories. Memories are recollected by associated reflections, such as Grandma and the story of Little Red Riding Hood. Now here comes Robin Hood. That reminds me of Robin Williams. Nanu Nanu! Remember? He was great in *Mork and Mindy*. That leads to *Aliens*. A bar scene, and we hear the music from *Star Wars*. Fight bursts out. The feeling of fear lingers. More than fear: danger. Danger is everywhere. Is that the *Titanic* sinking? It's a beach. Shiny, happy people. Oh, no!! Blood! A dangerous fish bites a swimmer at the beach! Jaws chewing crunchy breakfast. Crazy, we're in the middle of this mess. This is overwhelming. So much so that LI DOE's machine learning overcompensates and the algorithm shuts down. The WORL&D disappears as a giant curtain falls down, right onto LI DOE's head.

MENTAL TRAVEL: Hungary, 1980s
(What's behind the Iron Curtain, anyway?)

In the "Hairspray Eighties" of the Eastern Bloc, well behind the Iron Curtain, life is peachy as a high school freshman. That's when I single-handedly bring down the Communist Party. You know what? (Note to editor: Lisa, don't look!) I'll lowercase them: communist party. The disintegration happens on a Friday afternoon. We are supposed to meet and discuss the bright future of the young communist party, which we all know is a joke at that point. Instead, we turn the meeting into a musical trivia game. My friend Zoli and I pull together questions and facilitate a gameful contest for the rest of the crew. And that is our first and last "Communist" get-together. Two months later the communist party officially bites the dust, and their power disintegrates. Later on, the border with Austria opens, allowing East and West Germans to reunite through Hungary. They drive "Trabants," East German contraptions that move like cars, sound like cars, and disintegrate in rain like paper. Soon after, the Berlin Wall collapses. With that, the disintegration scheme continues. Same year, The Cure goes on a tour: first time ever in Eastern Europe! Oh, and guess what their album title is? *Disintegration.* And that is my first real concert.

As such, I conclude that I singlehandedly brought disintegration to the Iron Curtain with one musical trivia game that took place on an otherwise uneventful Friday afternoon. Music is more powerful than any regime. We're in the era of The Cure, Siouxsie and the Banshees, Depeche Mode. Talk about power! One of the most memorable examples of powerful simplicity of storytelling is Suzanne Vega's "Luka" and, of course, one of my all-time favorite tunes, "Tom's Diner." Between the iconic album release of *Solitude Standing,* and my in-person meeting with Suzanne at her twenty-five-year anniversary in a New York winery, she has sold over seven million albums and has been nominated for seven Grammys. "Tom's Diner" is one of those mysterious tunes I will never forget. And for those trivia fans out there: Suzanne is also known as the "Mother of the MP3," as her a cappella vocal track from "Tom's Diner" was used by German scientists to refine the algorithm for MP3. But enough of old memories.

For a long time, I was convinced that memories are like snapshots, like frozen moments you can recall at a later time. I imagined these events stored like computer files in folders; the faster the computer, the faster the access to the files. I was wrong. C'mon, it was the eighties.

As mentioned earlier, memories in the WORL&D are encoded nothing like a file in an isolated folder. When you store a piece of memory, a reflection of the outside world, the brain examines the item and finds already-existing categories or groups that the new item is associated with. Remember Grandma? She's a member of Women, Grandmothers, Pancake-makers, Storytellers, Smells, etc. When you remember "Grandma," all of these groups are retrieved.

The more often you remember Grandma, the faster your retrieval process. But! This is where I was way off in my thinking: it's not a snapshot, a static picture, you're retrieving. You're literally recreating the memory from all associated reflections. Grandma's picture is repainted every single time you recall her. What that means is that events that have happened since you last recalled Grandma may actually change how you retrieve Grandma. Like a painting you start anew every time. False memories, incorrect details, hop in and out.

One fascinating thing I learned from Kahneman, Fredrickson, and colleagues (e.g., Fredrickson & Kahneman, 1993; Kahneman, Fredrickson, Schreiber, & Redelmeier, 1993) about memories and emotions from the past may shape our decision-making in a strange way. It seems our retrospective assessments of past affective episodes mostly rely on 1) the moment of peak intensity of the experience and 2) the ending. At the same time, we neglect the duration of the experiment. In other words, you remember the height of the emotion and the ending of the experience, but not the time you spent in it. In a short trial, participants kept their hands in painfully cold water for sixty seconds. In a longer trial, participants did the same for sixty seconds, and another thirty seconds after. However, the water temperature was raised by 1° Celsius (still painfully cold). When asked which experiment participants want to repeat, the majority voted for the longer (sixty *plus* thirty seconds) exposure.

Now, what if these memories affect your evaluation of training or presentation the same way? What if participants mostly remember and form opinions based on the peak of intensity and the ending? I'm not talking about the effectiveness of a Level 1 evaluation, but how people assess in retrospect? Or, imagine customer service feedback! What if your score is mostly determined by the peak of the intensity of your conversation and the ending? Finish strong!

Have you ever had a dispute with a childhood friend about an event where you both thought the other one had lost their mind? It's crystal clear in your mind how the event played out. How come they don't remember?

In my high school years, we took a trip to the mountains of Slovakia. We know this because there's a picture of the group standing in the freezing cold on top of a mountain. That is a picture. Fact. A cue for the brain to remember. As strange it may sound, however, there's a debate going on right now among my friends about how in the world we got up there. Some remember climbing the maintain up but not down. Some swear we took the elevator (*lanovka*) to a point and then walked because of high winds. Some don't even remember going there.

Call to Mind!

Memories are unreliable! That's bad news for learning because using memories, as in remembering, is essential. Let's stop for a second and take a closer look at the word itself: remember. It hails from the Latin *rememorari,* which is literally "call to mind." To remember (haha) that remembering is a process of rebuilding a mental picture from scratch, let's pretend we don't know Latin, and look at the word from a different angle: re-member. Imagine the process of finding all "associations" Grandma is a MEMBER OF. Then reassess, and reassign her MEMBERSHIP again to new association, based on all experiences you have had. RE-MEMBERING Grandma creates a new wave of associations and memberships for Grandma. Some memberships will be reinforced, some weakened, some will be brand new. You may call this process a creative re-imagination.

If you don't recall Grandma for a long time, you may forget about her. Why do we have this forgetting flaw in our system at all? How to fix it? Why would the brain's system allow this gaping flaw? What if you could just remember everything effortlessly and forever? Well, it ain't gonna happen, so stop wondering about it. Forgetting is a crucial part of learning, the process that cleans out things we don't need and consolidates those that are important. At least, that's what folks believe here in the WORL&D.

Trouble is, what's important for you may not be important for your brain. I spent long years in higher education passing exams. They were all important. I earned two degrees, but why was it so hard to cram all that info in my head? Why did I have to spend so much time to make the info stick?

Whether cramming (aka pulling an all-nighter) is a good strategy for learning depends on your goal. It *does* work in the short term, allowing you to pass an exam, but a week or month later you might feel like you have no recollection of anything you studied at all. If your goal is performance in the long run, you must find ways to learn in a "spaced environment." Space out the learning; allow your brain to "digest." Remember to re-member! If you are the instructor, give people the opportunity to reflect on what they have learned. Reflecting is a complex process because it involves more than just remembering, it involves deep encoding. Give people references to what they already know. Reference points can work as re-membering hooks. The more hooks you provide, the most likely people will be able to recall.

One of the best ways to reflect is by asking questions. Not just questions, but *good* questions. Not just good questions but *the right* questions! If I have to sum up the successes in my career in one piece of advice for anyone in L&D, it would be this:

It's not about your tools, processes, or technology skills. Those come and go; the WORL&D changes all the time. It's about the ability to adapt both to the WORL&D and to the people in it. Your ability to adapt will most likely determine your value. And one of the essential skills you'll need for that is critical thinking, enabled by the never-ending practice of ASKING THE RIGHT QUESTIONS! And so, this book will return to this one question over and again:

"Am I asking the right questions?"

We need to foster a culture where people are encouraged to ask questions, then listen to and respect answers. Where they engage in meaningful dialogues. The notion of man vs. machine, as in single SILO learner vs. LMS, may not be the right framework for approaching and solving every problem of the future. One of the biggest mistakes we made with the revolution of eLearning was that we focused on technology instead of on the humans on the receiving end. We were more worried about completions, mass-loading learners, and administration of courses than the usability of the end product. In the early 2000s, conferences were buzzing around Learning Management Systems. *Do you have one? Which one?* We started shifting the performance issues from a human-centric to an IT-centric perspective. Later on, some of the most humongous systems integrated the whole talent management process as well. We've been asking questions like:

"How do you track learners?"
"How do you enroll learners en masse?"
"How do you create reports of time spent in course?"

The good news is, we found the answers and the solutions to questions like these. The bad news is, I'm afraid we've been asking the wrong questions!!

For example, time spent in a course? Aggregated into an annual giant number? We "delivered" value! Locking the screen until the audio ends will ensure that learners spend a long time in your course. But is it the value we should advertise? Has your company really achieved the compliance it needs when ten questions are answered at the end of a course? (Where, in fact, many people can answer those questions without taking the course?)

I want to salute those who instigated the Serious eLearning Manifesto[3] to lay down the guiding principles of eLearning design and development. One of the main instigators was Michael Allen, author and CEO of Allen Interactions. I grew up on Michael's first edition of *Guide to e-Learning*. So smitten was I that when the second edition came out in 2016, I wrote a review blog on it.[4] Michael Allen's book, just like any "training" project should, starts with business perspectives. Ultimately, the business doesn't care about number of clicks or action verbs used in a course. The business cares about outcomes. And that's where we should start as well.

Why Did You Pick the Hairdresser?

Imagine you have to choose between four hairdressers. They all post KPIs (key performance indicators) like total time customers spent in chairs annually and number of scissors clicks per year. Which hairdresser would you choose?

---

3   http://elearningmanifesto.org/the-authors/.
4   http://info.alleninteractions.com/michael-allen-hitchikers-guide-to-the-elearning-galaxy.

Well, truth is those numbers hold no value for me. I don't want to spend a specific amount of time in the chair; I want to spend the *right* amount of time in the chair. I want the hairdresser to ask me the right questions, and explain my options. If I come in with some crazy hair idea, don't just start cutting under tight deadline! I want her to say: Dude, I can do what you want, but let me ask you a couple of questions to make sure you get the biggest bang for your buck! I want them to ask me about my vision, my reasons, my goals, and then provide me with options for how to get there. That's the value I'm willing to pay for.

Without working their way through a few discerning questions, the hairdresser (or instructional designer) will never, ever say no and the client risks walking out looking mangled and feeling cheated. In the WORL&D, we must learn how to ask the right questions that then allow us to gently say no. Saying no doesn't mean defend and retreat. It means providing options that serve the needs and not the wants. Otherwise, you'll end up as an order-taker. And an order-taker can be simply replaced by an AI-powered robot. In fact, that's probably happening right now.

But, you might argue, you're an instructional designer; you're good at designing instructions. You love learning. You're passionate about methodologies, frameworks, brain functions, and everything related to the theory of learning. You're all about learners!

What if in the WORL&D learners didn't exist anymore? What if the Red King's lethal machine, the Scythe, put an eCurse on them all? What if everyone was frozen in time, stuck in the medieval era? What would LI DOE do without learners? What would the Last ID On Earth do without learners? Find a new job? Maybe become a hairdresser?

A Pawn Is Limited in Thinking

As LI DOE is mentally focusing on learners, he finds himself standing in the back of the classroom again in the SILO. The blackboard with the sketch of a Scythe is intact. While everyone is frozen in time, LI DOE feels it's a good idea to greet learners on slide 1.

LI DOE: "I am LI DOE. The Last ID On Earth. And I don't like it here. I want to go home!"

White Queen: "They can't hear you."

LI DOE turns around to see a tall woman wearing a white dress and a shiny crown. The White Queen moves swiftly to the blackboard.

White Queen: "They can't hear you or see you. It's the eCurse. They're frozen in old times."

LI DOE: "Who are you?"

White Queen: "I'm the White Queen. Welcome to the WORL&D through the looking class, LI DOE!"

LI DOE: "You already know my name! That's suspicious. How do I know it wasn't you who did this to them?"

White Queen: "Good question. I like how you think."

LI DOE: "I'm the Last ID On Earth. That's what I do in my old world. I think. I also ask questions and create courses."

White Queen: "Instructional Design is as much about courses and completions as interactivity is about Next buttons and mouse-overs."

LI DOE: "Do you often say random things?"

White Queen: "When you're a Queen, you can do whatever your objectives require. What are your objectives?"

LI DOE: "I want to go home, to the other side of the looking class. Which way is that?"

White Queen: "Well, let me ask you this: which way do you live?"

LI DOE: "I just said beyond the looking class. And I want my old world back! I don't like this change. I can't even move here! My muscles are not working."

White Queen: "Oh, in the WORL&D of chess, Pawns are limited in thinking and moves."

LI DOE: "I don't want to be a Pawn here. I want to go back to my old ID world."

White Queen: "There's only one way to return to where you come from. You must enter the Training Czar Heights."

The White Queen picks up a tiny piece of chalk. As she crosses the Scythe her fingers scratch the blackboard. That triggers bad memories in LI DOE's algorithm. By the second screech LI DOE can't hold it and runs to the board to stop the Queen.

LI DOE: "Stop!"

White Queen: "See, you can move."

LI DOE: "But I don't know how I did it!"

White Queen: "Pawns are limited in thinking."

LI DOE: "Here we go again. Are you related to Dory? You know, the fish from *Nemo*. She forgets things all the time?"

White Queen: "We all forget things all the time. But I'm the White Queen. Queens mean and remember every word they say."

LI DOE: "Okay, so how do I get this Training Czar place, smart Queen?"

White Queen: "You must be a Queen to enter. Pawns are limited in thinking, therefore they are not able to move worlds. However, if Pawns get promoted to Queen, their limitations are lifted."

LI DOE: "Queen? I thought you said you were the Queen."

White Queen: "I am the Queen, but you can have multiple Queens on the board at the same time."

LI DOE: "Good. Then promote me to Queen, and then show me where this Training Czar place is."

The White Queen chuckles …

LI DOE: "Something tells me it's not going to be that easy."

White Queen: "Unfortunately, only the Red King can promote you to Queen."

LI DOE: "And where do I find this Red King?"

White Queen: "Downtown. In the shadows of Training Czar Heights. It's the Western part of the WORL&D. But I wouldn't go there without the magic mojo shield."

LI DOE: "I feel like I'm reaching my cognitive overload here. Okay, you know what? I'm a Pawn with limited thinking, so why don't you just tell me my learning objectives, so I can go home."

White Queen: "The WORL&D is under the eCurse by the Red King and his powerful Scythe. Learning is stuck in the medieval era. Myths such as learning styles are dominating our brainwaves. Legend has it that one day a hero arrives, a hero who can break the eCurse. A hero who will not only break the spell but will also lead the L&D folks to the light. Today, you are that hero, LI DOE. You are the One. Collect all six missing pieces of the Magic Mojo Hexad first, and then face the Red King and his Scythe."

LI DOE: "Let's cut to the chase. Learning objectives: Collect the six missing magic mojo pieces. Get promoted to Queen. Return home. Got it! Let's go!"

Awkward moment.

LI DOE: "I can't move my legs. How do I go?"

White Queen: "Oh, learning objectives. We use performance objectives to move here: you use your mind to travel places in the WORL&D, and your body will follow. Remember, everything starts with a mindset change. Like this!"

As the White Queen disappears, LI DOE looks at the sketch of the Scythe on the board.

LI DOE: "Like this! Perfect. Meanwhile, I'm stuck in this stupid SILO! In a dark SILO with a stupid Scythe! I wonder if I'll ever see the Sun again."

"Instructional Design is as much about course completions and time spent in courses as interactivity is about Next buttons and mouse-overs."
— *Rabbit O'Reg*

LI DOE squints at the bright Sun. She's not the dark SILO anymore. She's standing at the edge of the tiny SILO island. A ferry is ready to leave for the main WORL&D, carrying a giant piece of cake. The loudspeaker calls for last-minute passengers. LI DOE makes a mental move to hop on before it's too late, but a White Rook appears from nowhere and blocks him, shaking his head dramatically.

White Rook: "You can't click Next until the audio is over."

The Rook goes on rhythmically nodding. LI DOE realizes the Rook is listening to music.

LI DOE: "I'm not clicking anywhere. I have learning objectives."

White Rook: "Talk to me, baby!"

LI DOE: "Huh?"

The Rook starts dancing. LI DOE notices the wireless earphones. LI DOE gestures to turn the music off.

LI DOE: "I need to find the six missing pieces of the magic mojo shield for the learners before it's too late. I need to get on that ferry."

White Rook: "Did you say learners? Are you a Carrier?"

LI DOE: "No, I'm the last instructional designer on Earth from beyond the looking class. I'm here to break the Red King's spell on learners."

White Rook: "Learners? I'm a Rook, and I can tell you, there's no such thing as learners here."

LI DOE: "What do you mean there are no learners, Rook? Am I too late?"

White Rook: "Too late for what?"

LI DOE: "Are they gone? Was that the Red King's Scythe?"

White Rook: "Don't say that name! You need to calm down, and think about your thinking. Learners and gompies are not real."

LI DOE: "I don't understand! What do you mean not real?"

White Rook: "Oh, Pawns. Drops in the Ocean."

LI DOE: "Limited thinking. I know."

The ferry takes off with the cake …

LI DOE: "Why do I feel like I'm always missing the boat?"

White Rook: "Are you a patient?"

LI DOE: "Patient? No, I'm an ID."

White Rook: "When you go to a doctor, would you call yourself a patient?"

LI DOE: "In my old world? Yes, but that's a different story."

White Rook: "So, when do you change into being a patient? Do you call yourself a patient at home before and after a visit?"

LI DOE: "At home? No, I don't call myself as patient. Only when I see the doctor."

White Rook: "Okay, so for the doctor, you are a patient. But for anybody else, you're not."

LI DOE: "Kind of. Look, I am on a mission. Learners …"

White Rook: "So, in your old world, you're a human before and after visiting the doctor, and a patient during the visit. If the doctor doesn't know you before, and will never see you after, when you're a human, how would they know what you need as a human? They would just give some pills to a patient, and move on to the next? That would be silly."

LI DOE: "Okay, I gotta go. I'm not a doctor. I'm an ID. And if you can't help me to achieve my learning objectives, tell me where to go. I'm a pawn with limited thinking and I can't move fast, I'll need some time to get there."

LI DOE turns around toward the SILO but won't move an inch.

White Rook: "In this WORL&D, you go where your mind is, not where your body wants to."

That makes LI DOE turn around.

LI DOE: "You sound like the White Queen. Related?"

White Rook: "How is that relevant?"

LI DOE: "Relevant? I just wonder if everyone here is born a smart-ass or it is a learned behavior!"

White Rook: "Mr. Funfetti attitude! Let me tell you a story."

LI DOE: "I don't care about staying relevant here. I want to go back to the old world, where learners are alive and things are normal. I don't like this change. I hate being relevant."

White Rook: "In this WORL&D, there are no learners. Humans have a life before, during, and after anything they learn. Most of them don't want to learn; they want to do their jobs better, faster, easier, whatever. As for the Red King and the Scythe, if you're the One, I assume you have a storyboard on how to break the spell."

LI DOE: "That happens later. I'm just analyzing right now."

White Rook: "Well, then analyze this: without the Magic Mojo Hexad shield of instructional design, you won't stand a chance against the Red King here in the WORL&D."

LI DOE: "You guys keep repeating yourselves. Normally, I wouldn't need any mojo, but if you insist, you can get me one. Fine."

White Rook: "Get one? You don't just get one. You build one."

The Rook zips away in a straight line. Then zips back again with a hexagon shield.

White Rook: "Here, this is your core shield. It has the six missing traits on the front, map on the back. Collect the missing six traits before you face the Red King."

LI DOE: "So, if I really wanted to find those missing traits, how would I find them? And where the heck am I right now?"

The Rook flips the shield. The inside has the map of the WORL&D with a flashing green spot showing the exact spot LI DOE is standing.

White Rook: "How to find them? Be curious! Ask the right questions."

Suddenly, wolf howling echoes from distance. The White Rook quickly hands over the shield. The bright Sun's reflection on the shield blinds LI DOE for a second. And with that, the Rook zips out of sight. LI DOE regains his eyesight and looks at the shield.

LI DOE: "Ask the right questions? What questions?"

Asking the Right Questions

The profession of instructional design, just like L&D itself, is going through a transformation. The question is not whether changes will happen, but how fast will they happen. And with the changes, the right question to ask is how to stay relevant. Some say it's an evolution (slow and steady); some say it's a revolution (fast and continuous); and for some it's time to leave the baggage behind and jump (disruption start-up).

No matter which group you identify with the most, they all agree that the notion of instructional design as "content creation" won't have a long-lasting future.

"Learning is no longer a controlled substance only happening under L&D supervision in an LMS lab. Lifelong learning happens with or without L&D."
— *Rabbit O'Reg*

Are you experiencing budget cuts in training? Are you at the table early on, when major decisions regarding design happen? Are you ahead of the business, informing them on knowledge and skills gaps, or do you barely have the time and resources needed to get the course out on time?

If our role remains stuffing content into courses, administration of courses, and reporting course completions, then sooner or later AI and automation will take care of our problems. And it will take care of us, too. And when that time comes, the Red King's Scythe will harvest on its own, without human interaction.

Does It Float?

LI DOE picks up the shield. It's surprisingly light. Very light. Like Trabant light.

LI DOE: "That's paper, not a shield! I wonder if it even floats."

The moment LI DOE realizes what he did, it's already too late. His mind is somewhere else he would never want to be.

Storytelling: Floating Some Ideas

The Ocean is calm today. Only an occasional wolf howl breaks the silence. LI DOE is floating, holding tight to the shield. The answer is yes, it does float.

LI DOE: "Great! First, senile Dory, and now what, brutal Bruce? Oh, no. I'm not thinking of Bruce. I'm not thinking of sharks. Hey, Rook! I changed my mind! I'd rather be relevant than shark food. I'm ready to be rescued! I'm really curious about that story now, too! I want to stay relevant!"

Staying Relevant

To stay relevant in the WORL&D, let's float some new ideas: what if we returned to the basics? What if we stopped chasing buzzwords like AR/VR, AI, microlearning, gamification, blockchain, whatever. There is time for those as well, but first let's settle on core values by asking some (right) questions:

Who are we?

What do we think about ourselves?

What do we think about the WORL&D?

What does the WORL&D think about us?

How do we think in the first place?

What's *your* story of who we are? What do we bring to the table? L&D has never been about content; it's always been about humans. You might call them "talents" in your WORL&D. L&D should tell the story about humans, how they grow and develop to achieve more than they would have ever thought. L&D's story should be more about the conductor who becomes invisible between the audience and the orchestra. About someone whose value is not measured by how long the musical piece takes, but how the experience impacts the short walk in the parking lot after the event, or the watercooler conversations the day after. User experience is what brings the audience to fill out the room. The best conductors become invisible during the performance, literally "conducting" the experience by connecting the orchestra with the audience. Letting the music tell the story, creating the experience itself, is more memorable than any drag-and-drop in the WORL&D.

One of L&D's challenges today is showing the value to the business. Showing the value is not an easy task because the value L&D creates is not in the course content, it's in people's minds. It's invisible, yet actionable. It's the knowledge, skills, and behaviors we ultimately help change, and we should capitalize "HELP." We're not changing anything. We facilitate the change. If your story is about the content you create, the length of training hours you provide, and the number of completions you count, your story will most likely end as a drama or a thriller. While automation can replace us with tools to create content, we still have the advantage of creating good stories that resonate with the audience on an emotional level. The path to staying relevant in the field of learning and development may not hinge on new technology or buzzwords, but rather on our ability to conduct to engage, motivate, and inspire humans.

Storytelling is a powerful tool to engage, motivate, and even inspire humans. And so, the art of storytelling is a tool we must master for survival.

Mistakes to Avoid When Telling a Story

Storytelling has been with humanity for a long time. It's a powerful way of conveying ideas and stories to engage, motivate and even inspire others. But storytelling and storywriting are not the same! They require different skill sets. It's like playing music and writing music. Just because you read a lot of stories doesn't mean you can write a good one. So, what are the some of the top mistake we may make when writing a story?

MENTAL TRAVEL: Massachusetts, 2000
(Where I write a story. And it's bad. Really bad.)

On a rainy morning in our Cambridge apartment, right off Harvard Square, I decide to write a screenplay. Now, this is not such an uncommon momentary lapse of reason among people in the United States. There are so many spec (not commissioned) screenplays out there that you have a greater (far greater) chance of being hit by lightning than of having your screenplay made into a movie. After some initial research on how in the world to even write 120 pages, I complete my first masterpiece in a mere three months. Storytelling is as easy as playing the piano: just hit the right key at the right time with the right pressure. I submit my masterpiece to a competition. The result? We'll get to that later. For now, let's look at some of the rookie mistakes new writers (and instructional designers) often make when creating a story:

1. On-the-Nose Dialogue

This is what on-the-noise writing looks like in a screenplay:

```
INT. KITCHEN -- DAY
Gigi enters the kitchen with two grocery bags in
her hands, and a car key in her mouth. Joe, half-
dressed, sitting at the table munching on dry ce-
real. Gigi stares the wide open cabinet door.
                    GIGI
          I told you to shut the cabinet
          doors a hundred times. This makes
          me feel like I'm not respected in
          the house. You know this behavior
          reminds me of my ex husband. I'm
          afraid I'm going to react as if you
          were Greg.

                    JOE
          I am sorry that an open door makes
          you feel like that. It's just an
          open door. I will close it soon.
          You know I love you, and I'm not
          Greg.
```

This would never happen in a movie. Why? Because people don't say what they mean, especially when they're emotionally charged. It would probably go like this:

INT. KITCHEN -- DAY
Gigi enters the kitchen with two grocery bags in her hands, and a car key in her mouth. Joe, half-dressed, sitting at the table munching on dry cereal. Gigi stares the wide open cabinet door. After a quick glance at Joe munching, Gigi head butts the cabinet door to shut it.

Joe glares at her.
                    JOE
        I'm not Greg.

When you create a dialogue for eLearning, don't give words to your characters. Give them personality, and then encourage them to speak. Don't put words into their mouths; put feelings into their hearts. Throw them into a work situation with competing priorities, and then let the words spill out naturally. Let the audience read between the lines. They will be much more curious about what and why your characters are saying (or not saying). Without curiosity, there's no engagement.

2. Unnatural Speech

Creating good dialogue in a movie is not easy because you're not actually writing a real dialogue. You're writing an imitation of a dialogue that looks and sounds like one, but only contains elements the story needs to move forward. What looks good on paper often does not translate well when you say it out loud. In fact, writers often end up redoing or ditching whole scenes because they just don't work. How do you know if the script works? READ IT OUT LOUD (letters capitalized in writing often feels like you're shouting)! Let me shout this out again: READ THE SCRIPT OUT LOUD!!

What looks good on paper, or even sounds perfect in your head, may not work at all when spoken. Always read everything out loud! For learning, the script is often created by the SME. It "covers" all the content. When you read it out loud, it sounds unnatural, like a teleprompter or a marketing brochure. Especially in a dialogue! People don't talk like a marketing brochure. You can easily kill your story by adding bad dialogue. One more tip for video (less applicable for audio only): imagine the dialogue takes place in a completely empty room except for two people standing back to back who can't see or hear each other. They're only told when to read their lines.

If your conversation makes sense this way, your script is dead. What it needs is CPR: context, people, and reactions. Every believable conversation has context, from place to props to background noise, and all of those things should support your story. People don't read lines in real life; they interact with each other and with their surroundings. In other words, don't say what you can show. Fiddling with a pen can express much more anxiety than actually saying "I'm a little nervous today." And finally, reactions! React to each other's points, not only what they say, but how they say it, or, even better, what they don't say. Silence can do amazing things with empathy.

3. Unrelatable Characters

Often, beginner screenplay writers add all kinds of twists and turns to make the story exciting. The thing is, it's not the twists and turns that make a story stick. It's more likely how your audience can relate to the characters. If people don't care about a character, they don't care what happens to them. That's why it's rare that an affluent, well-educated, healthy, athletic, raggedly handsome white guy is the main hero to save the world. Unless it's a thriller and he risks losing all of it …

For learning, create scenarios and characters your audience can directly relate to. Don't make up a sunshine scenario where all the customers are nice, they all know their account numbers, and express why they're calling in HR-appropriate, marketing-approved full sentences. BORING... That's just not real. Add accent, add noise, add mumbling, add tone, add attitude, add whatever makes it real.

Oh, and the good old excuse, "We don't want to provide bad examples!"? The power of storytelling is that you learn from mistakes others make. By NOT providing "bad examples" you're actually depriving your audience, keeping them from learning. Those bad examples will happen for real, whether your stakeholders like it or not. If your stakeholders or SMEs insist that they don't want to show bad examples, ask them if these bad examples might happen in real life. If they say yes, then ask them where they would prefer people encounter them, in a safe place with constructive feedback or in real life with no support? That said, you must also demonstrate the desired behavior!

4. Long (as in l-o-o-o-o-ng) Scenes

There's a simple rule in screenplay writing: keep a scene only if it drives the story forward. "Kill your babies" means get rid of all extra fluff and nice-to-know; keep only those scenes that directly drive the story. Yes, even if it's great and you love it like your baby. Believe me, cutting is REALLY hard.

You should not only cut entire scenes out, but also trim the ones you keep. You should enter every scene AS LATE AS YOU CAN and leave AS SOON AS YOU CAN. Here's an example: if a boss is about to lay off one of his direct reports, the scene would not start with the boss calling the person to come in to the office, shutting the door, having a chat around the weather, etc.

The scene would start with both of them sitting in the office, staring at each other. And silence. Then the direct report says something like: "What about my new house? We just closed yesterday ... My wife ..." And the boss would turn to his computer as he gets an instant message: "Happy hour tonight?" There's your moment to show (not tell) the audience what kind of boss he is. The emotional reaction would let the audience know what to expect from his character.

For learning, create a scenario that includes only elements needed for the learning. Scenarios are powerful, but keep them as short as you can. Start with the core problem, then let participants explore the situation and learn more. Use nonverbal cues, and maybe include a notebook function in the eLearning where they can keep important info.

5. Lack of Beats

A story works only if it evokes emotions. Movie scenes you remember years and years later, when you have no clue what happened before or after, those contain "beats." Why? Because they left an emotional footprint on you!

A beat in a screenplay is an extremely important moment, when something absolutely critical happens. Most of the time, it's a dramatic revelation both for a character and the audience. As a writer, you use this sparingly, but you must have these in your story to prove compelling. A good example is the movie, *The Sixth Sense* (screenplay by M. Night Shyamalan).

How could you forget the scene when the wedding ring drops on the floor, and our hero realizes he's dead? That's a beat. You never forget it. I bet Bruce Willis will never forget it. And if you noticed, Bruce doesn't say: "Oh, I just realized I'm dead."

You can create the same experience for the audience when you think in beats that lead to performance goals. Moments when the human, while interacting with the content, suddenly has a revelation, a beat they can never forget because it leaves an emotional footprint. And let me tell you, I've never seen anyone emotionally driven by bullet points on the screen.

I am guilty of committing all of the above (especially long scenes) in my first screenplay. Are you curious about what happened to my screenplay? We'll get there later.

MENTAL TRAVEL: Cambridge, MA/Philly, PA – 2000s (Curiosity and job interviews.)

Being in the States only for a couple months, finding a job is not the easiest task without any credit history, work history, references, etc. First of all, I'm not even sure what jobs I should be considering. In January I start looking at open positions on Monster.com that are related to computers and learning. I quickly land on "Technical Writer" jobs. How do I get me one of those?! Curiosity drives me to download the trial version of FrameMaker and RoboHelp. I learn them in a week. In fact, I prepare my presentation in RoboHelp for the Tech Writer position at Unica Corporation (today it's part of IBM). Curiosity led to an interview and a job. It was a great opportunity to work with smart MIT people in a small company where I could make a difference. I also learned that technical writing isn't my sweet spot; I'm too creative for the restrictions.

In 2007, I apply to an Instructional Systems Designer job at Comcast. They send me a course to review: "What would you change?" Curiosity drives me to check the source code of the application to track down the original authoring software: Lectora. I haven't used Lectora before, so this is the perfect time to download the trial version. I rebuild the whole course in a more engaging format in two days, and send it back to the hiring manager. I stay there for almost nine years.

Curiosity is the never-ending engine fuel. If used properly, you can leverage the energy for troubleshooting, innovation, design, creativity … you name it. The first step is to obey the urge to ask questions. Do your research, and play what-if games with it in your head as if it was your friend.

Curiosity Is Your Friend

A rescue boat from the City of Curio is approaching. LI DOE waves frantically with one hand, while holding on to the floating shield with the other. As the boat gets in range, the White Rook picks up his bullhorn to address LI DOE:

LI DOE: "Finally! What took so long for a Rook?"

White Rook: "The more you take away from me, the bigger I get. Who am I, Funfetti?"

LI DOE: "You said you were a Rook. Hey, I want to stay relevant before Bruce gets here."

White Rook: "Wrong answer, Funfetti!"

LI DOE: "Okay, can we play this in the boat? I've been floating here for a while and this mind traveling is not working out for me."

White Rook: "You have exceeded the three tries. Your progress has been reset. You must start from the beginning, Funfetti."

LI DOE: "Start from the beginning? What does that mean?"

White Rook: "Just follow your curiosity, Funfetti!"

The boat turns around and leaves LI DOE floating behind …

LI DOE: "Just follow your curiosity? You're so unbelievable!"

Follow Your Curiosity!

Follow your Curiosity! I'm not talking about deep, life-coaching advice here. As part of NASA's Mars Science Laboratory mission, Curiosity is the largest, and most capable rover ever sent to Mars. Curiosity is meant to answer the question: "Did Mars ever have the right environmental conditions to support small life-forms called microbes?"

More importantly for us, Curiosity has several cameras taking pictures 24/7. That means you can see what Curiosity sees on the Mars!! How awesome is that for us curious people?

As an instructional designer, curiosity is your greatest friend. If you can make someone curious about any topic, they're hooked. Without that, you can apply all nine Gagne's events, or gamify your Next button with thousands of badges and likes, and it probably won't make a difference in the long run. I'm a curious person. Whenever I meet new IDs I ask them how they decided to become one. Here are my absolutely unofficial results:

How Does One Become an Instructional Designer?

Two ways: accidentally or intentionally. For those going to school to become an instructional designer, the path is clear. And there are great programs for that. For everyone else, there's Cammy Bean's book, *The Accidental Instructional Designer*.

MENTAL TRAVEL: Hungary, 1970s
(Where one learns about instructional design.)

As a young human, I don't really know what I want to be. Luckily, growing up in Hungary in the 1970s, we have a handy-dandy official book of professions in the school library. In eighth grade, I go through the book to try to picture my future. None of the professions in the book impress me.

To understand the situation, imagine a Communist regime pushing blue-collar workers to become the new elite for decades. All the jobs in the book involve somehow getting really dirty. I've nothing against rolled-up-sleeves work, but there is not a single computer in any of the pictures. Meanwhile, I am learning how to code in BASIC. I know coding is an everyday thing nowadays, but imagine learning a programming language without two things: the internet or a computer.

Our elementary school has two computers, which you can sign up for a couple of hours a day. One is for those who play games. The other is for coding. I'm torn, but decide on coding. A couple of hours a day is not enough to type in and troubleshoot long lines of code. The code has to be bug-free by the time we get to the computer. How do you write code and debug without a computer? On paper.

I write the code down and run it in my head. Basically, I am the CPU. After each round of bug fixing, I copy the new, better code (there is no copy-paste), line by line, on paper again. I'm sorry for all the trees I killed.

I'm Not a Geek. Do I Really Need to Learn Coding?

Some say coding is for geeks. For me, there's a difference between coding and programming. Programming is a mindset fostering analytical thinking. It's the process of building logic before writing code. Once the logic is in place, you code. You choose the language you use. That's the physical aspect. Just like in the WORL&D, everything starts in the mind (programming) before you can move (coding). Debugging is the process of finding out the difference between the intention (your programming logic) and the actual (coded execution). A bug is not a mistake, as Mr. Robot says:

> "A bug is never a mistake. It represents something bigger. An error of thinking.... That makes you who you are."

For an instructional designer (even if you don't code), the ability to be able to debug, analyze, isolate and resolve root causes of complex problems is a HUGE advantage in the field. It teaches you critical thinking and quick troubleshooting.

Programming may not even involve actual coding anymore. Scirra's Construct 2 (and 3 just came out) game engine is a great 2D application to build games without writing code. What you're building is logic. You must be able to translate your vision into a coherent logical map. In the future, robots powered by artificial intelligence will be able to write code for themselves, but humans will still need to provide them with expectations. That's programming.

Authoring tools such as Articulate Storyline offer basic elements of programming: variables, triggers, and conditions. Using the power of programming makes you a superhero among heroes. Again, programming doesn't start with typing code. It starts with the familiar skill we've talked about many times here: the art of asking the right questions.

But that's not why I decide to become an instructional designer. That's just why I get one of the most important temp jobs in my life, a job that brings the a-ha moment of a lifetime.

MENTAL TRAVEL: Hungary, 1989
(Where I learn about the value of knowledge.)

After two weeks at college studying to be an architect (this is a story in itself), I decide to run away from anything that involves straight lines and firm rules. That is when I am hired to orchestrate one of the most exciting New Age miracles in the history of Hungary: the first free, democratic elections after forty years of Communism. In 1956, the Soviet Union's Red Army marched in and stayed in Hungary "temporarily,' for like forty years (no kidding, they had the official name of "Soviet Union's Red Army Temporarily Stationed in Our Country").

Anyway, as I turn eighteen, I become eligible to vote in the first real election in forty years with more than one person on the ballot in each race. (I'm not sure how nail-biting it was to choose between one Communist candidate on the ballot before, but who knows.)

The job I'm hired to do involves sending encrypted voting information through the online system. First time in the Eastern Bloc! At this point, we have like eight new major political parties. Each of them sends a representative to the room where I am working with the IBM 386 computer (that nobody is allowed to touch except the eighteen-year-old). It's election night. I have an IT guy sleeping on the floor with a motherboard, ready to rebuild the whole computer in case any part should blow up. I have a professional data entry person typing the results. But for the most part, all eyes are on me, and all ears are focused on the noise the computer makes when it goes online.

As I said, my temp job is to send the encrypted voting data to the command center over the internet. We're talking dial-up, baby! Nobody, and I do mean nobody, in the room has the faintest idea what it means to preformat the hard drive to create a non-DOS-compatible partition to avoid hacking.

How exciting! Every decent modern country is represented in the watch group to monitor the first free elections in Eastern Europe. The headquarters are in Budapest. That's where the press is staring at the monitors all night long. Little do they know that they're going to learn their first two Hungarian words that night: *Nincs Adat.*

Nincs Adat displays on the monitors all night long. It means "No Data." Again, whoever thought it was a great idea to experiment with full-blown electronic data transfer in a country that hasn't seen a fresh banana in forty years I'm not sure ... but that's not *my* problem. Me and my IBM 360 computer in an empty room in a tiny town, I'm adding value by doing what I'm supposed to do: sending data.

What Is the Value of Your Service?

Here's what I learned that day/night about value: people don't pay for the time it takes you to complete a job. People pay for what it would take THEM to complete the job. People pay for the VALUE of your service!

It's the story you tell that makes a difference. That's when I decide that my story will be about using computers and emerging technology, and, most importantly, working with people who need applications to solve their problems. Because the faster you learn new technology, the faster you can figure out the application of it in real life.

I'm all for technology. I have an engineering degree. But I firmly believe that technology is never a solution. It's a vehicle to support your journey toward your destination. But first you need a destination.

Don't let technology drive your solutions! Design the solution first, then find the right technology. It's like coding and programming. You don't start writing code for a software application until you know the VALUE the app will bring to users. It's all about USERS, CLIENTS, CUSTOMERS!

For now, let's just remember that the value of an instructional designer is not in the course content they create. If you can solve a "training problem" with a checklist, do it! If you aren't convinced, check out Connie Malamed's article "The World Needs More Checklists."[5]

Today's business problems are complex. Why do we think they can be addressed by ONE training/learning solution? We've trained the business very well when they need an ILT or an eLearning. The best-trained even know how long the eLearning will be, before we ask a single question about their business problem.

I encourage you to use Cathy Moore's Action Mapping® (or similar tools) to analyze the root cause of why humans aren't doing what they're supposed to be doing. An effective solution for a complex business problem probably have multiple component, and it is not a one-size-fits-all learning solution. Assuming that learning (let alone training) is the solution will most likely derail you from the beginning.

---

5   http://theelearningcoach.com/elearning_design/isd/
checklists-for-learning/.

If you think in the "learning bubble," your solution will be a learning course. Before you get to learning, let's think about the end: measurement. Then think backwards: measurement -> desired behaviors -> performance goals -> learning/performance support -> (maybe) training.

Here's a rundown of a sequence of questions we often ask:
- What is the business goal?
- How are you measuring success?
- Who are the people who can make impact to achieve that goal?
- What should these people be doing to make impact?
- Why are these people not doing it?
- What type of obstacalities are we looking at?

Of course, the process is a little more complex, but this is a good start to asking the right questions. And yes, "obstacalities" is not a real word. I made it up for my sessions. When your brain hears the word "obstacle," you focus on barriers and problems. "Obstacalities" may not have any prior bad associations, and so it may mitigate your limitations and bias. (Of course, right now it is merely a hypothesis, as no scientific evidence supports my approach.)

Obstacalities: How to Beat a Shark?

When LI DOE spots the white fins, he knows the right question to ask. He just can't remember it, as the name "Bruce," from *Finding Nemo,* is on the top of his mind.

LI DOE was right, these mental moves weren't working out too well yet. Somehow, the more pressure he was under, the harder it became to focus on to be somewhere else. Meanwhile, the shark started circling around her.

LI DOE: "Hey, Bruce! I don't want to die as a Pawn!"

The White Shark emerges in full.

LI DOE: "This is it, the apocalypse!"

White Shark: "My name is not Bruce. My name is SHELSTÖDISBORG. Welcome to the new age! And by the way,

Pawns don't swim. You're a liar. You're a juicy Queen."

LI DOE: "Right, Borg! Think! If I was a Queen, I would swim!! I wouldn't just float here, right? I'm a Pawn."

White Shark: "Deep in my bones, I know Pawns are supposed to sink and drown, not float."

LI DOE: "Well, I'm just holding on to this thing. That's why I'm not sinking."

White Shark: "If you're a Pawn, you're supposed to have limited thinking."

LI DOE tries hard to think of a better place to be. Just then the White Shark jumps out of the water to strike. Its wide open jaws are about to cut LI DOE in half. LI DOE closes his eyes and submerges into the water. The Sun's reflection on the shield hits the beast, and the White Shark misses the strike. LI DOE pops up, gasping for air, only to see nothing but the calm Sea and the intact shield.

LI DOE: "Wow! Two words: you coward. Borg, you're so unbelievable."

MENTAL TRAVEL: Hungary, 1984
(Where I do something bad. Really bad.)

I'm going to give you two words. I want you to draw something mentally. Something you think of when hearing these words. Do it quick. Once you start "drawing," do not lift your pencil. Ready?

Bűvös Kocka

Never heard of a Bűvös Kocka? No wonder. It didn't exactly take off under its original Hungarian name. Ever hear of a Rubik's Cube? Same thing. Magic Cube, as it was originally called, in Hungarian is Bűvös Kocka. Ernő Rubik invented this unbelievable magic around 1975, hence the name Rubik's Cube.

I am ten years old when the Communist regime sends a message that we must collect toys to send them to (if I remember correctly) Nicaragua to show our solidarity. No explanation. No nothing. Bring your favorite toys, kids, and send them away. We are children but not stupid. This is in no way volunteerism or solidarity. We are volun*told* to bring in a toy to send to a country we have no clue about. Anyway, I bring in a Rubik's Cube. I figure this would be a really good fit for a country in the middle of a civil war.

Please, Forgive Me!

Now, I officially beg for forgiveness! If you were the child who received my Rubik's Cube (although, I doubt that the Communist regime actually shipped the toys) and have been desperately trying to solve it ever since, you were doomed. In my momentary lapse of reason, and selfish frustration as a child forced to give away his toy, I hereby confess that I took the Rubik's Cube apart. I did. And then I put it together in a deliberately funky way, so that it could never be solved. And for that I am truly sorry!

Have you ever taken a Rubik's Cube apart? It includes tons of tiny little pieces. Every little cube is actually a moving piece around the core, which is in the middle. Fascinating structure. What does it have to do with workplace learning?

Mr. Rubik didn't set out to invent a toy. He worked at the Department of Interior Design at the Academy of Applied Arts and Crafts in Budapest. He had a business problem to solve:

The structural problem of moving the parts independently in 3-D without the entire mechanism falling apart. (You'll see in this book I use the term "business problem" to refer to the actual, most of the time measurable, workplace challenge outside the learning bubble.)

The Rubik's Cube solved a business problem, and also became one of the world's best-selling toys ever. The point is, we should always focus on the goal, the outcome, and not the content, engagement, or fun.

If your focus is on designing course content, you will design and build a course, regardless of whether a course is the right solution. Let's shift our focus from content to problem-solving! Sometimes that will mean designing a solution allowing people to grow their knowledge or skills, which they will then apply to resolve problems. But SOMETIMES it will mean we are working directly with the business to resolve problems by offering solutions that have nothing to do with course-building per se. And SOMETIMES it will be about motivating people who already know what to do and how. If you're an instructional designer, and all you do is create how-to guides and courses on solving the Rubik's Cube, no matter how good your skills, your job is in danger. That can be done by robots. In fact, they're already doing it. Google them!

Always look to the Rubik's Cube! We're not in the business of making toys, coloring cubes, or building how-to play courses; we're in the business of solving problems that often includes knowledge and skill gaps!

The rest of this chapter will introduce LI DOE to the six traits that may help problem-solving in the WORL&D. But right now, there's something else on LI DOE's mind.

The City of Curio

LI DOE's mind was still contemplating how to tell the heroic story of defeating Borg, the White Shark, when the mental power of beating all odds triggers a sudden move. He finds himself in the center of the abandoned City of Curio.

This mind travel is not bad, thought LI DOE.

Except, without full control over his thoughts, the physical moves seem somewhat arbitrary right now for her. For one last moment, LI DOE turns back to reflect on all the things she learned about the SILO.

As I said, nobody really knows how the SILO works. The best explanation folks can come up with is a model. There are already people who claim the last model, the information processing model, is just not working anymore. Folks will always be looking for more accurate, better models. If you're interested in another model of the mind, check out Robert Epstein's "The Empty Brain," in which he argues that your brain does not process information, retrieve knowledge or store memories. In short: your brain is not a computer.[6]

Dancing Queen

With a swift diagonal dance move, the White Queen, playing a tambourine, dances into the main square in the City of Curio.

White Queen: "You come to look for a King?"

LI DOE: "What King? Red King? I swear, this Dory thing will drive me nuts."

White Queen: "You are the One! I feel the beat from the tambourine. I am the White Queen, digging to meet you! This is the City of Curio. We have a long way to go to collect all six missing traits. Can you jive?"

LI DOE: "Jive? I'm the same LI DOE you met in the SILO. Look, I got my mojo thing, see? As you said, I just need to find the six missing traits. Do you remember?"

White Queen: "You're mistaking me for the other White Queen. I used to be a Pawn, just got promoted to Queen by the Red King. I'm having the time of my life! Let's start with Critical Thinking. Legend says it's hidden somewhere on a giant stump in the Hills of O'Rious. To get there, you must pass the busiest folks in the WORL&D: the order-takers."

LI DOE: "You sound like a badly written audio script. Do you ever actually have a dialogue? Can you listen?"

Suddenly, a wolf howls, and it sounds like right next door. The White Queen shivers, anxiously looks around.

White Queen: "We need to hurry! Here are the six missing traits:

1. **Critical Thinking** (from order-taking to problem-solving)
2. **CREAM** (CReativity, Engagement, And Motivation)
3. **Adaptive Resilience** (The Art of Bouncing Back)
4. **Human-Centered Design** (Design and Game Thinking to move from content to context)
5. **Social Impact** (work-out-loud personal-brand relationships)
6. **Myth Bunking** (The Science of Learning, Artificial Intelligence, Evidence-Based Practicality, Knowledge-Skills-Attitude)"

The White Queen spins around to see the source of the howl. A Red Fox stares at her. A slight breeze hits the White Queen. She looks up in

---

6   https://aeon.co/essays/your-brain-does-not-process-information-and-it-is-not-a-computer.

the sky and screams in fear.

LI DOE: "A fox doesn't howl!"

White Queen: "Run! Run! Tessellate!"

From out of nowhere, a Red Scythe appears in the sky and chops off the White Queen's head. She lands on the sidewalk, motionless, like a lifeless chess piece. More Red Foxes appear from the shadows and drags the White Queen away. The Scythe loops around and flies right at LI DOE. LI DOE ducks at the last second.

LI DOE: "Tessa? Who's Tessa? And why is Tessa late?"

Tessellate Your Inner Hexagons

The choice of shape for this gameful storytelling memoir was obvious: the largest regular polygon that tessellates.

The hexagon shape is popular in games for several reasons. One of them is tessellation. Tessellation is tiling a surface (such as a gameboard) without gaps in between tiles. There are three regular polygons that can do this: triangle, square and hexagon. The advantage of using a hexagon is that you have the largest space to work with, and there are six ways to move around from one hexagon to another. This gives you more choices and faster moves (one of my favorite board games, Settlers of Catan, is a great example).

Enter your inner hexagon! Imagine your potential career as the wild, open space. You can be anyone in the WORL&D with the right knowledge, skills, and motivation, at least in theory. In reality, your success also depends on space and time. To be at the right place at the right time can help you tremendously. The hexagons you're laying down represent your career, which you are building by tiling the space around you. The more you have on the board, the greater your chance of landing on a job you desire. Timing is also crucial. This is why we're using hexagons, to travel fast from place to place. The more hexagons you have on the board, the more resilience you build against any unknown changes.

The gameful adventure starts with a single hexagon in the middle of nowhere. This is your base. Each side of the hexagon is a trait. A trait is a combination of knowledge, skills, and motivation. Your base hexagon is the foundation of your career in the WORL&D. This adventure memeoir is about building and strengthening your core, inner hexagon. I will challenge the way you think, engage you in activities via storytelling, motivate you to complete some real-life challenges, and hopefully inspire you to continue building out your gameboard with new, exciting tiles that can take you to wherever future brings.

But let's not think that far ahead. Let's first focus on your Level 1: building your magic mojo hexagon shield (your base, that is).

IRL Challenges:

"We need a course" is common request we hear (most of the time it's also a last moment call to action). Next time someone asks you for training, ask if you could as a couple of questions to make the course most impactful:

- What is the business goal?
- How do you measure success?
- Who are the players (people who can make an impact)?
- What are they not doing that they should be doing?
- What holds them back from doing the right thing?
- What type of obstacalities are they facing?
    - Internal Knowledge (do they need to remember? really?)
    - External Knowledge (what resources do they need?)
    - Skill (how will they practice?)
    - Motivation (they know what they need to know, yet they're still not doing it; why?)
    - Environment (what is the stuff you can't control?)

(For the whole methodolody behind Cathy Moore's Action Mapping, read her new book, *Map it*. For now, let's do baby steps. Just by sorting out what kind of issues you're facing, is a good start.) Use this information to focus on where direct impact of learning is the most likely along with existing resources that can be used for performance support.

Focus on ACTIONS (observable actions or decisions), and not things people need to know.

Chapter Two

CRITICAL THINKING
(FROM ORDER-TAKING TO PROBLEM-
SOLVING)

Pursuit of Trait 1/6: Critical Thinking

Where Are We?

The mental path from the City of Curio toward the Hills of O'Rious leads through the Land of the Order-Takers. Hills of O'Rious is the highest point of the island. This is where ancestors of Hill O'Rious, the White King and White Queen, are supposed to live and rule today. Instead, the White Queen is hiding from the Red King, while the White King has supposedly retired to run a small business enterprise under a pseudo name. His whereabouts are unknown at this time.

The best view of the island comes at a price. It often stumps visitors by challenging them to think about their thinking before entering the region. It may sound strange at first, but again, this is the land of the whimsical.

Thinking about your thinking is a process that has helped many to gain residency and move up on stump levels here. No one is allowed to enter Hills of O'Rious without first solving a puzzle that requires thinking about their thinking. The Order-Takers, folks who have not yet passed the thinking puzzle test, are always running behind. Be careful! Three tries and you join their ranks.

The Order-Takers are the most reliable folks. They act quickly, without asking too many questions. In the Order-Takers' culture, asking questions would project insecurity. They're always the last to know what to do, therefore planning is not their forte.

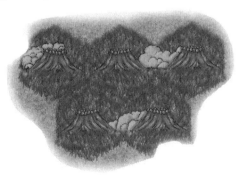

Walking along the narrow mental critical path, LI DOE arrives to a building that looks like a fast-food drive-through. The road is blocked by a gate; there's nowhere to go. On the window, a handwritten sign says: "The Pawn Shop has moved to Creative Cave." Behind the glass window, a Dispatcher is busy with monitors. The orders are coming in fast.

LI DOE is about to ask where to find the Critical Thinking piece of the Magic Mojo Hexad when the Dispatcher addresses him directly:

Dispatcher: "Speak when you're spoken to."

LI DOE: "I'm from beyond the looking class. I've beaten a shark."

Dispatcher: "A-ha. Mr. Worldwide, just wait for a moment until the gates are open."

LI DOE sits down on a bench to wait for the gate to open. He picks up a magazine to flip through. The article on connecting the dots resonates with him.

Order-Takers: Connecting the Dots

We have a compliance issue. Our people are not connecting the dots.

We have straightforward guidelines and strict deadlines but our people are not connecting the dots. No lines, see?

We need a dot awareness module and a gamified dot connecting course. We were thinking of maybe PacMan. It would be fun. With 5 COL questions at the end. By next week.

Somewhere in the WORL&D, people are not connecting the dots...

Imaginary conversation follows in the article:

Bad ID: "PacMan is a good idea. [*Not really.*]. Let me ask you a couple of questions to make sure we're going to find the best solution for you. So, you said your people are not connecting the dots and you want them to connect them, correct?"

Client: "Yes. We have an SOP in place with straightforward guidelines. People are not following it. Also, I'm having huge turnover."

Bad ID: "How many dots are we talking about? I'm trying to measure where we are today."

Client: "Lots."

Bad ID: "Lots. [*That's not a number.*]. So, if we could reduce those un-connected dots to less than lots, you would call it a successful solution?"

Client: "Well, if we could reduce it from lots to some, it would be excellent."

Bad ID: "Got it. And when do you want this to happen?"

Client: "Soon."

Bad ID: "So, we can establish the business goal as being to reduce the unconnected dots from lots to some by soon."

Client: "Sounds good. Do you think you can build the PacMan by then? It has to be branded. And legal wants to see it frame by frame."

Bad ID: "Now, before we get to PacMan, why do you think people are not connecting the dots? What holds them back from connecting them?"

Client: "Does it matter?"

Bad ID: "Well, the solution would probably be different, say, if your people don't recognize dots, right? If they don't know what a dot looks like, they won't connect them. Or, if they don't know how to connect dots, they would hesitate, right? Straight line? Color? Permanent marker? Maybe they don't have the tools. Or it could be that they just don't see the point."

Client: "Dots. Not points. These are dots. How long do you think the seat time will be for the PacMan? My people are busy building pyramids and I need to make sure production doesn't suffer."

Bad ID: "I understand, and we're going to makes sure our solution will be the most efficient to achieve your goals. So, do you think maybe we could talk to some of your people about why they're not connecting the dots?"

Client: "You mean those who are not connecting them?"

Bad ID: "Yes, to inquire as to the reason ..."

Client: "They're dead. Not connecting the dots calls for capital pun-ishment. That's why I have huge turnover."

Bad ID: "So, your people are aware of the consequences of not con-necting the dots, which means they have a pretty good incentive to do so, yet they are still not doing it?"

Client: "Yes, there are two reasons why you die here. One is not con-necting the dots. Two is asking too many questions."

Bad ID: "[*Oops!*] I think I have everything for the PacMan game."

Moral of the story: Asking too many questions leads to bad client experience. Don't be a bad ID!

LI DOE laughs out loud. Just then, the gate flings open and a White Knight carrying an envelope screeches to a halt. The Dispatcher rips up the envelope.

Dispatcher: "You! C'mon! Time is money!"

And with that, he slides a forty-slide PPT deck of FAQs to LI DOE. As LI DOE's trying to indicate that he's not an Order-Taker, an alarm goes off. Code Blue emergency policy goes into effect. A White Pawn grabs the slide deck from LI DOE and runs with it. No questions asked. Running as fast as a Pawn can run. The lights go off. The Dispatcher falls back into his chair.

Dispatcher: "Phew, that was close. You must learn how to plug and play without wasting time asking questions!"

LI DOE: "Not sure what plug and play is but I'm looking for the first missing piece of the Magic Mojo Hexad. Do you know where I can find Critical Thinking?"

Dispatcher: "A-ha. You want advice? Don't waste your time. Time is money. You won't pass the confirmation of learning!"

LI DOE: "I've beaten a White Shark named Borg today. Bring it on!"

Dispatcher: "C'mon, sharks are in water, Pawns are not."

LI DOE: "Maybe I started a new trend?"

Dispatcher: "Pawn with an attitude! C'mon, live for the moment! Keep trying new things and you'll fail. You really want to fail? Go ahead. Find the Truth-Tellers Colony."

LI DOE: "The Truth-Tellers Colony?"

Dispatcher: "Oh, another question! Just take the Pawn away from here!"

The White Knight knocks on LI DOE's shoulder.

White Knight: "Why did you pick the shovel?"

LI DOE: "Shovel? What shovel? I didn't pick any shovel. Are there any sane creatures in this new WORL&D?"

The White Knight grabs LI DOE and off they're teleported to ...

"Why Did You Pick the Shovel?"

Traveling with a Knight is an experience. The constant hopping would test any ID's stomach. LI DOE is mostly concerned about his head. He feels unbalanced circuit circulations, labeled "dizziness" in his long-term memory. Finally, they land on a giant stump, so big you can't even see the end. On hop-path, they arrive to a fork where a giant ant stands, dressed as a White Bishop.

White Knight: "Two ant tribes live here. The Truth-Tellers and the Liars. When asked a question, the Truth-Tellers always tell the truth, while the Liars always lie. You want to go to the Truth-Tellers Colony to pick up the Critical Thinking piece. On the path, you will arrive at a fork at the hanging tree. One of the roads will lead to the Truth-Tellers, the other to the Liars. A White Bishop will be standing at the tree there, but you won't know from which colony. You'll have a chance to ask one question to find out which way to go."

LI DOE: "Hmm… I'm not sure about all the future tense. Aren't we already here?"

White Knight: "I can't think straight. I think in hops. Anyway, one question to ask! There can be only one!"

LI DOE: "One question?"

White Knight: "One. If you're not asking the right question, you'll end up working for the Order-Takers a year before you can try again."

What Would You Ask?

Remember, Truth-Tellers always tell the truth, Liars always lie. What ONE question would you ask to learn which way the Truth-Tellers Colony is?

My ONE question: _____?

To solve this challenge, most people need to do something they might rarely do: think about their thinking. Examining and challenging the way you think is the fundamental pillar of Critical Thinking.

Why is Critical Thinking on the Magic Mojo Hexad? Why is it important as a skill for us learning professionals to survive?

In *Critical Thinking: Tools for Taking Charge of Your Professional and Personal Life,* Richard Paul and Linda Elder point to adaptability in a changing world.

"Critical thinkers have a distinctive point of view concerning themselves. They see themselves as competent learners. They have a 'can do' vision of their own learning. They do not see opposing points of view as a threat to their own beliefs. They see all beliefs as subject to change in the face of new evidence or better reasoning. They see themselves as lifelong learners."

Critical Thinking starts with the basic idea of thinking about your own thinking. You must take a moment, without multitasking, and focus on why and how you make decisions; think about the logic you apply, the bias you may have, the filters (social, age, geopolitical, gender) you use to "make sense of the world." Let's freeze this moment as we return to the problem of the Truth-Tellers.

Reading the Truth-Tellers' problem, your initial reaction is probably something like asking about the weather or the color of the sky. Based on the answer, you would know whether the White Bishop is a Truth-Teller or Liar. You would ask them which direction to go. Knowing whether the answer is true or not, you're on your way. So, with two questions, the problem is easy to solve. But how do you ask one question and learn two things: the tribe and the correct way to go?

You may feel you're stuck. Let's stop and think about the logic we're applying to problem-solving here. Is there a flaw in the logic itself? If you're like most people, you assume that you must know whether the White Bishop is a Liar. And that's exactly why you get stuck.

Do we really care where the ant is a Liar? You probably think *yes, otherwise how would we know if the answer is correct,* right? In reality, you only care about which way the Truth-Tellers Colony is, not whether the ant is a Liar. The challenge is that the answer would be different from a Liar and a Truth-Teller, and that's causing your issue. But what if the answers were the SAME from both a Liar and a Truth-Teller? Would that help?

And your brain goes: how could they be the same when one of them is lying? And that's exactly the QUESTION you must ask yourself! How could the answers be the same? Could they be the same?

Is it possible to ask a question where both tribe would show you the way to the Truth-Tellers Colony? It's only possible if their answers (before lying) are different. That means you have to ask a question where the CORRECT answer actually depends on the tribe. That way, the Truth-Teller would give you the correct answer, while the Liar would give the incorrect, but since he lies, he would give the opposite, the correct answer as well.

I was speaking at the eLearning Guild's DevLearn conference in Las Vegas when I posed the same puzzle to the audience. After some thinking someone came up with this approach:

"What would an ant from the other tribe say when asked where the Truth-Tellers Colony is … and whatever the ant says, you would go the other way."

Let's see if that works! First, let's assume the ant is a Truth-Teller. In that case, the other tribe would lie, so a Truth-Teller would point me to the wrong direction. Check. What about a Liar? For a Liar, the other tribe would point to the right direction, but since this ant is a Liar, he would change that to pointing to the wrong direction. Check. See? Both of them are sending you to the wrong direction. Which means, you choose the other way no matter what.

Asking the right questions starts with examining how we think. While the solution we found works, you may wonder if that's the simplest solution. With that let's return to LI DOE, who's focusing on the right question.

White Bishop: "Why are you coming to the tree?"

LI DOE: "Well, I have limited thinking …"

Suddenly, a random memory pops up in LI DOE's mind. This is new. He didn't have this feature before. The algorithm threw up a random memory with the White Queen. And LI DOE knew exactly what the right question to ask was.

LI DOE: "Which way do you live?"

Which way do you live? Now, the answer from the Truth-Teller is the correct one, and the answer from the Liar would lead to the Liars Colony (where they're from), but since they lie, they would point to the opposite way, which leads to the Truth-Tellers Colony. So, no matter where the ant is from, the answer would lead to the Truth-Tellers Colony.

White Bishop: "Wow! Strange things did happen here, but no Pawns have ever passed this test!"

How Does the Story of the Truth-Tellers Relate to L&D?

Have you ever worked with SMEs who wanted to add a ton of information to a course because the learners "need" to know it? Imagine if an SME wants a guide on how to get to the Truth-Tellers Colony and insisted that it include the history of the island, descriptions of the two tribes, major historical events and names, etc. But your goal is simply to get to the Truth-Tellers Colony. Once you're there, you may want to learn more about their things to see, but that's a different goal, which means it's a different guide.

Solving the Truth-Tellers and Liars problem can be difficult because of your beliefs. You believe that you must know the tribe in order to interpret the answer. Therefore, you're looking into solutions with the assumption/filter that you must know their tribe first. That road leads to frustration. Without questioning your beliefs you will never solve the problem.

Critical Thinking forces us to question our beliefs. In fact, changing behavior for good cannot be done without changing existent beliefs. The steps we've seen while solving the problem above is part of reflective thinking. According to Richard Paul and Linda Elder, we are all born unreflective thinkers. Critical Thinking is a skill you develop to be a reflective thinker, and it starts with the idea of thinking about thinking.

MENTAL TRAVEL: Elementary School, 1980s (Where I think about my thinking.)

In elementary school I have to attend the after-school program until my parents get out from work. The best way to describe the after-school program is like a detention center. You sit in dead silence. Only the clock is ticking. You're supposed to work on your homework and learn. Mind-boggling how teachers think this is the best way to educate young human beings. It is during those hours one day that I calculate how many hours I waste in my life sitting in a quiet room, staring at the clock. I've hated ticking clocks ever since.

In retrospect, there is one advantage to the situation: I am thinking a lot. Thinking about thinking. If you never question your assumptions and beliefs, you see the world in black and white. It's you or them. You believe what you see, and you see what you believe. If someone disagrees with you, you get emotional because it's obvious they're wrong, they just can't see it. In extreme cases you make up your own alternative facts. Anything that supports your beliefs is magnified and generalized, while everything that does not fit into your belief system gets labeled as "exception" or "suspicious lie."

The Truth-Tellers' Colony

The Truth-Tellers Colony is a neat place with a buzzing social life. Telling the truth all the time is not simple. At the entrance gate, a large sign warns you to leave your ego and bias behind. A guard White Bishop ant from the top of the gate shouts to LI DOE:

White Bishop: "Why did you pick the shovel?"

LI DOE: "Shovel? What's up with this shovel again??!"

White Bishop: "That wasn't not the right question to ask."

LI DOE: "Why, are there any questions I *should* have asked?"

The gate opens. LI DOE frowns but grabs the opportunity.

"What Other Questions Should I Have Asked?"

Asking the question above is a powerful way to wrap up a meeting. It serves a double purpose. For one, you show you care. You open up the floor to the unknowns, because obviously, you couldn't ask about something you're not even aware of. But it also forces the participants into Critical Thinking. When you ask this question, you often get a moment of silence and wondering eyes. RESIST the temptation to keep talking. Your participants are engaged in a recall process. They're synthesizing and summarizing all that was said first (nobody wants to repeat a question that has already been discussed), then search for related information. They think about their thinking. *Was there something we missed in our logic?* After ten to twelve seconds they might say: "No, I think we've covered everything." Occasionally someone will come up with "The only thing I can think of ..."

In either case, all that is left for you to do is summarize the takeaways and next steps.

Why is Critical Thinking part of the Magic Mojo Hexad? Because asking the right questions is the fundamental core of what L&D is about, or *should* be about. Stakeholders rarely come to ask what they need; they ask for what they think they want. Asking the right questions comes from experience. And sometimes it takes a long time to ask the right questions. For example, it took twenty-five years for Dr. Gazzaniga to a solve a decade-old mystery about the brain.

"Why Did You Pick the Shovel?"

In Dr. Gazzaniga's experiment, a split-brain patient was shown two pictures: the man's left hemisphere saw a chicken foot; his right hemisphere saw a snow scene. (The brain's left hemisphere is where the language skills are centered, while the right is more holistic—it does not have words for what it sees.) Then the patient was shown an array of pictures, which both hemispheres can see, and he was asked to choose related pictures. The man chose chicken with the foot and shovel with the snow. So far the experiment went as expected. And that's when asking the right questions was critical. Dr. Gazzaniga asked a simple question:

"Why Did You Choose These Items?"

And the answer was a complete surprise. The chicken goes with the foot. That was expected. But for the shovel, the patient said it's to clean out the chicken shed. Dr. Gazzaniga called BS. What happened here was a complete BS story made up by the left brain. An explanation that would "make sense." Yet, it's complete BS. Since the left brain didn't see the snow, the patient subconsciously chose the shovel but had a completely different explanation as to why. And here comes the left brain making up a story. In subsequent studies the pattern emerged: the left hemisphere gets whatever information it gets (whether fact or instinct) and tells a tale to the conscious awareness. It makes shit up. Literally.

"It only took me twenty-five years to ask the right question to figure it out," said Gazzaniga.

So, remember this question: "Why did you pick the shovel?"

"W-H-Y" are the most powerful three letters in the WORL&D. Use them often; use them wisely.

MENTAL TRAVEL: Client Meeting, 2010ish
(Where a kickoff call turns interesting.)

I'm on a discovery call with clients about issues they see with their bill. I'm talking about your basic cable bill here. Said client requests training on how to explain the bill, as customers are finding it hard to figure out what they see. For the first ten minutes of the call with multiple stakeholders, I don't even say a word. They're discussing right off the bat how long the eLearning should be: ten or fifteen minutes. Ten minutes is easier because it's hard to get agents off the phone, but it might not be enough because the last module was fifteen and it "barely covered" what they need to know. They agree on a twelve-minute WBT with five COL questions at the end. Then, finally, I speak. I ask why. Why do they think customers are having issues with the bill? How do they know this is an issue? How are we measuring success?

There is silence. The not so convincing answer? "This is a very common reason why customers call." I push more. *How* common is it? They say they will pull the data and we can meet again.

Two weeks later they contact me and explain that this actually used to be a problem but now, with the new redesigned bill, it is no longer a common reason for customer calls. If you're an order-taker, this would have been another waste of twelve precious minutes for thousands, and tens of thousands of dollars lost in productivity.

MENTAL TRAVEL: Hungary, 1993
(Where I RISC my life.)

I am teaching computer technology to freshmen at college. One of my favorite topics is how early application of Critical and Design Thinking lead to one of the least known (outside of the computer geek club) yet of the most powerful innovations in computer technology.

In the 1980s a new processor appeared that revolutionized the market. If you're not a computer geek, you may have never heard of RISC. Before RISC, the prevalent approach to computer chips was to shift complexity to hardware. In fact, the complexity grew so quickly that designers needed to have multiple processors to work together. Then came RISC. The reason I wanted to explore this mental travel is because it's not about technology. This story is about Critical Thinking and shifting mindset.

It started with asking the right questions: Were we using those complex instructions built in current processors? What instructions were used more frequently than others? What if we simplified the instructions and made execution faster?

Using simplified instructions would pose a problem: making up complex instructions from simple ones would take a longer. Complex instructions then would have to be done through multiple single ones, which makes the code size bigger. But! Asking the right questions helped again:

How often are complex instructions used? Could we build a single chip with reduced instruction set that shifts burden from the hardware to software? What if we reduced the most time-consuming task of accessing external memory to store and load values? What if we researched how commonly memory is used and add "memory" on the chip itself to store limited information? These, and other questions about ACTUAL usage pattern, led to the revolutionary RISC processor. In modern speak, the combination of Critical Thinking, Design Thinking, Research, and Creativity led to a counterintuitive yet more powerful approach.

In instructional design, we often make decisions with SMEs and stakeholders on what stays in a course and what does not. Often we argue back and forth on what modality is the best to achieve the performance goals. In practice, there's limited budget and resources we face all the time.

Now, imagine if we made decisions based on actual research data. For example, when designing a curriculum for onboarding new hires: imagine you had a list of tasks a worker will perform and the frequency, complexity, and risk associated each task. Then you could focus on the most frequent and/or most critical tasks first. As for memory access, the most time-consuming exercise employees do is searching for information or duplicating existing information. Give them intuitive resources, a checklist to work with, and a buddy (maybe an AI-driven bot as well). Onboarding is a process, not a fun event.

Let's shift from hardware to software. Let's remove all unnecessary burden from the brain to software that allows employees to find information when they need it. Let's design our workplace to support performance, where learning happens as needed! At the same time, let's give humans a safe place to explore. We all know telling is not training, and that people learn from their mistakes. Yet the first thing to cut from learning is usually the interactive exercise and the challenges where they may fail. Why? Because often that's how the decision-makers learned, or maybe they don't want to deal with complaints. Often, they believe that telling people what to do is the same as providing performance support. How do you change that opinion?

I'm sure if you're an instructional designer, you have all the theory and research you need, probably right in your back pocket, to convince your stakeholders. The challenge is that business doesn't care about theories, abstracts, long essays, or white papers—not even action verbs or Bloom levels. When your SME tells you that learners don't need scenarios because they have all the SOPs (standard operating procedures), they just have to read them, you're looking at an unreflective thinker. You can't win the argument unless you move the SME from that unreflective level. Otherwise, you just argue back and forth, as you can see in online discussions. People must question their own beliefs before they can change their minds. So, the question is not how to change someone's mind but how to make them think about their thinking first. And thinking about your thinking is what Critical Thinking is about.

The Unreflective Thinker

The challenge with unreflective thinkers is that they actually think they don't need to think differently, and that others are just plain wrong. "If we uncritically believe what we were taught to believe, these beliefs are likely to become part of our egocentric identity. When these beliefs become our identity, they affect the manner in which we believe."

Following are the six stages of Critical Thinking:

Stage 1: The Unreflective Thinker (we are unaware of significant problems in our thinking)

Stage 2: The Challenged Thinker (we become aware of problems in our thinking)

Stage 3: The Beginning Thinker (we try to improve, but without regular practice)

Stage 4: The Practicing Thinker (we recognize the necessity of regular practice)

Stage 5: The Advanced Thinker (we advance in accordance with our practice)

Stage 6: The Accomplished Thinker (skilled and insightful thinking becomes core)

What does this have to do with learning? If your level of Critical Thinking is not on the same level as that of your audience, you're going to have a shouting match without any progress. You must know your audience, and adjust accordingly. Why is Critical Thinking a huge advantage for L&D? Again, Richard Paul and Lina Elder argue that critical thinkers have a distinctive point of view concerning themselves: they see themselves as lifelong learners. Lifelong learning is a must in the age of rapid change.

Are you having issues with engagement? There you have it. You may have an issue with unreflective thinkers who believe "they already know everything." That's why it's crucial to challenge humans; to show them better, easier, more compliant ways of accomplishing their goals. By just telling them what to do, you're throwing peas on their unreflective wall.

How to Talk to an Unreflective Thinker?

Let's say your SME says that you'll have to lock every screen of the eLearning until learners hear the complete audio. You must also make sure the same text is displayed on the screen. Otherwise they won't pay attention. You probably know that forcing people to listen to a slide while reading the same long text on the screen is bad. Really bad. However, if you say that research says it's actually hindering learning when people see and hear the same thing on the screen, here's what your SME is going to hear: you're questioning whether the topic is important. Why? Because in the SME's mind the intention and means are the same. The topic is important, learners must pay attention, therefore we need to force them to listen. If you question the means, you question the motive.

How to convince the SME then? You must find common ground. Paraphrase the motive: "I agree, this is really important for the learner to remember. I understand we want to make sure that happens. Forcing learners to listen to the audio seems one way to accomplish that. How about if we find some other ideas to reinforce the importance of paying attention? For example ..." Now you're separating the motive and the means. Reinforce the motive, and then brainstorm on the means.

Early in my career, I was having a hard time listening while analyzing a problem with stakeholders. Since I had a solid background in solving learning challenges at the workplace, it was so easy to stop listening and switch to solutioning. Solutioning has its place, but if you let your mind settle on a solution in the middle of the discovery, you'll find that everything else said afterward perfectly "makes sense" for the solution. Why? Because you really want to believe that. When in fact, it may not at all. Cathy Moore's Action Mapping process (starting with the flow to decide if it's a training problem at all) is a great way to start practicing this mindset. Discovery is digging deeper and deeper for foundations; it's not about building the house yet. Watch your thinking to learn more about how you think. The more you practice Reflective Thinking, the easier it gets to spot biases, mistakes, or false assumptions in your way of processing information.

LI DOE watches the first trait, Critical Thinking, lighting up on the shield. Her AI circuits are tingling as she feels accomplished. Mission #1 is complete.

White Queen: "Congratulations, LI DOE! Creative Thinking is now part of your Magic Mojo Hexad. From now on, every day, set aside just minutes at the end of the day to think and reflect. Unplug, and focus on one situation that happened during the day. Reflect on your thinking, your reactions, your decision-making. As you do this every day, you're growing the trait of Critical Thinking into a habit."

LI DOE: "I don't have time for reflecting, right now. What's next?"

Test Your Memory!

Without going back to find the information: do you remember where the Pawn Shop moved?

IRL CHALLENGES:

1) Where do you see your Critical Thinking level currently?

Stage 1: The Unreflective Thinker (we are unaware of significant problems in our thinking)

Stage 2: The Challenged Thinker (we become aware of problems in our thinking)

Stage 3: The Beginning Thinker (we try to improve, but without regular practice)

Stage 4: The Practicing Thinker (we recognize the necessity of regular practice)

Stage 5: The Advanced Thinker (we advance in accordance with our practice)

Stage 6: The Accomplished Thinker (skilled and insightful thinking becomes core)

2) Start thinking about your thinking daily! Pick a situation at the end of each day, and think about it. Spend 10 minutes just thinking:

What was the situation?
How did you react?
What made you react the way you did?
What would have been a better, more rational reaction?

Chapter Three

CREATIVITY, ENGAGEMENT & MOTIVATION
(FROM PAGE-TURNING TO MIND-BLOWING)

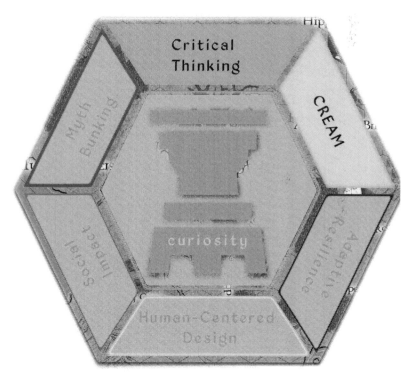

Pursuit of Trait 2/6: CREAM

Where Are We?

The Creative Cave (where the Pawn Shop has moved) is a place to relax, rejuvenate, and, surprise, be creative. This is the place for new things to come to light. Both good and crappy ideas are welcome. The Creative Cave is used by many wise WORL&D folks as a place—*the* place—to exercise mindfulness. There's limited space inside, and therefore the rules are clear: your body can only enter the Creative Cave if your mind is already there.

Inside the cave, you can touch the dense darkness, and smell tranquility. In fact, it's so dark there that you may lose your sense of time and space. Humans often report hearing whispers, seeing insights, even feeling wet drops of saltwater from the Sea, as they go with the Flow. It is one of the mysterious places connecting the Hill and Sea brothers. The Red King often sends critical thoughts to those entering the cave. Thoughts like "this is not going to work" or "I'm not good at this," even "this is stupid." You must stay calm and ignore these thoughts, otherwise your mind leaves the place and, you know the rule: your body must follow.

While the Creative Cave is located in the North of the WORL&D, you can actually get here from anywhere. Remember, it's the mind that needs to enter first! And if the Red King tells you your mind is limited to what you do and where you are physically at the moment, don't believe a word that he says! Everyone has a couple of minutes a day somewhere to listen to their echo of their own silence.

Too busy? Unplug. Look up. You may see the WORL&D in a different light. Watch this clip on YouTube when you have a chance: "I have 422 friends, yet I'm lonely."[7]

LI DOE and the White Queen stand in front of the closed Pawn Shop. A note is hanging on the door: "ARIA says: think of me."

LI DOE: "Who's ARIA? Is she your friend?"

LI DOE tries to open the door …

White Queen: "Remember, you can't enter until your mind is there.

---

7   https://www.youtube.com/watch?v=Z7dLU6fk9QY.

Think of her."

LI DOE: "Of ARIA? Who's she? Does have the key to the Creative Cave?"

White Queen: "This is the Creative Cave. Purge your thoughts! Open up your mind to enter. Be aware, the Red King is going to try all kinds of distractions to make you question your creativity."

LI DOE: "This sounds like a lot of work. I prefer the opposite, just play."

White Queen: "The opposite of play is not work."

The White Queen gestures to be silent. A wolf howls in the distant. That's enough for the White Queen to swiftly disappear before a sinister dark cloud appears on the sky in a shape of a Scythe.

"The opposite of play is not work, it's depression." — *Jane McGonigal*

MENTAL TRAVEL: DevLearn, 2015
(Where we learn about CREAM: CReativity, Engagement And Motivation.)

When speaking at conferences, I often ask the audience to raise their hands if they think they are creative. Not too many hands go up, usually. When we discuss with the "creative ones" how they know they are creative, the conclusion often leads to the discovery that others label them creative. The "Creative" label is given for ideas that nobody else thinks of. Ideas that come from thin air, seemingly, that is. For "outsiders," creativity seems to manifest from thin air, like a lightning strike without a warning. That is a big misconception holding back many humans out there from applying creativity. Creativity, just like the four seasons, has its cycle. Forcing creativity may lead to frustration. To understand how to harness creativity, we need to go deep inside the Creative Cave.

Is Creativity an Addiction?

For me, the best way to describe my creativity is to compare it to addiction. You learn to live with it. The more you understand how it works, the more control you have over it, but you can never get rid of it. The more you control you have over it, the easier it is to help others be creative. While creativity may have many definitions, let's look at from the pattern recognition perspective: creativity is the ability to see connections before they exist (in other people's eyes).

As you recall, from the SILO, all memories are stored by neurons and in their elaborate connections, called synapses (at least based on the information processing model). When you recall a memory from the past, these neurons fire in various patterns. Their connections light up. The human brain has the ability to merge and rearrange these synopses, and so create something that didn't exist before by firing different patterns. This is what we call imagination. The ingredients are all in the brain. How do they get there? Curiosity is a key driving force. Curiosity feeds the brain with ideas. How do you force your brain to come up with new ideas? Good question. You don't.

The brain does an amazing job finding these new paths if you let it! The moment you sit in the regular brainstorming meetings on Thursdays from 3pm to 4pm, it just won't happen. All of your ideas are crap? Then you go home, frustrated, as a creative person who couldn't contribute. While in the shower, it hits you! The idea, I mean. "How could I not see this solution before?" Congratulations, you just stepped out of the way and let your brain do what it does best without you trying force it.

The reason you didn't see the solution before is that you tried to force your "logical brain" to come up with a new path. All you did was just running in circles firing the same paths, while expecting something new as a result. In fact, the harder you to try to get away from a path, the more difficult it gets. I'm not thinking of a white elephant!! There it is. The white elephant. Which leads to frustration. Do you ever have issues remembering someone's name? An actor? You literally see this person in front of your eyes, even quote his lines, and still you can't remember his name? The harder you try, the worse it gets. It's because you're forcing your brain to run through the same neuropaths over and over again, expecting the answer to be different. Then you say "I draw a blank." You give up. On the way to the bathroom in the bar, you see the waiter bringing out a burger and you SCREAM from the top of your lung: "Bacon! Kevin freaking Bacon!"

What just happened? You let go. You let your brain work its magic. You let the control go. The first cue (burger with bacon) triggered your brain to search for associations, and bang! Kevin is right there with the bacon.

There are excellent books on exploring how the brain MIGHT operate. In *Thinking, Fast and Slow*, Daniel Kahneman refers to the two modes of thought: System 1 (fast, instinctive, and emotional) and System 2 (slow, deliberate, and more logical). In *Design For How People Learn*, Julie Dirksen uses the elephant and the rider metaphor from Jonathan Haidt to describe similar relationship between the two modes. Similarly, in *The Writer's Process*, Anne H. Janzer builds on the Muse and the Scribe to explain how to maximize your brain's creativity to write well. (In the WORL&D, you may remember the founders, Sea O'Rious and Hill O'Rious, who had similar tendencies.) Whatever labels you use, we'll look at my suggested four steps of coming up with creative ideas in a little bit. The secret of the process is not thin air; it's the ability to follow the cycle of creativity and to leverage the strength of each phase. Creative people do this naturally.

MENTAL TRAVEL: Hungary, 1995
(Where I get creative.)

I'm teaching Hungarian language and culture to Peace Corps volunteers in a small town in Hungary. This is back in the time when people are expected to be smarter than their phones. Hungarian is one of the most challenging languages in the world. To ease that challenge, I am spending long hours coming up with lessons that deal with conjugation and other crazy grammar things that once you master, you can't really use anywhere else in the world. Now, this is an experiential learning exercise, as we have three groups and three teachers. We're rotating teachers. I'm looking for something to bring us together, something engaging to help ease the grammar drills. Then one night, in the middle of nowhere, an idea pops in my mind: an old blind and lame prince. (Basically, the opposite of Prince Charming).

In Hungarian folk culture, number three is a traditional element. There's always three trials before a Prince can marry. So that night, I decide to merge the folklore and grammar into a play. I write a "grammar" play for the three groups. Each group has a scene, followed by the finale with everyone on stage at the end. Now, to the conjugation. The story is about a King who wants a Prince to marry the ugly Princess. So the old blind and lame Prince arrives. However, he has to go through three trials. With each trial, he has to beat a wicked grammar witch of the forest. There you go, an arm wrestling conjugation trial. After a successful attempt, the witch honors a wish. And that's how the old blind and lame Prince gradually becomes a young, Elvis-footed man with 20/20 vision. Which makes him change his mind about marrying the Princess at the end. Hence the title of the play: *Such Is Life (Ilyen az Élet).*

The point is, there were no grammar exercises or drills involved. It was all about humor, social connections, and a common vision. Did they practice conjugation for the play in front of the whole group? You bet. And I bet some of them, if they ever read this book, will still remember: *"Apám, hull a hó."*

Creative Cave

LI DOE is sitting in a dark, empty cave. He's trying to think of ARIA, whoever she is. A White Pawn appears in front of him. LI DOE is about to say hi, but the Pawn indicates to be silent. The Pawn points to his head. Another Pawn arrives. Then another two. The four Pawns form a line. And they mime YMCA with their hands.

LI DOE indicates he has no idea what they're doing. Each Pawn shows a letter: A-R-I-A. LI DOE nods, and follows the Pawns down a narrow path. The path leads to a hidden creek. The Pawns get into a boat. LI DOE hesitates for a second. The Pawns show another four-letter word: F-L-O-W. Seeing as how the creek flows into the darkness, LI DOE is not sure if it's a good idea. Finally, he hops in the boat, holding his shield tight.

How Does Creativity Make Its Magic?

How to harness the Creative Cycle? David Rock's awesome book on how the brain works, refers to this cycle as the ARIA model.

The ARIA Model

In *How the Brain Works,* Rock walks you through the ARIA model (Awareness, Reflection, Insight, Action). This is exactly how it feels when you come up with a creative idea. Here are the brief phases (read the book more details):

Awareness

This is the phase where you state the problem and activate the prefrontal cortex of your brain. Simplify the problem with a short statement: I want to explain variables, conditions, and triggers in a simple way in Articulate Storyline.

And here comes the hard part. Do NOT try to solve this problem. That would not result in a new creative approach. Go with the flow; let it "sink."

Reflection

This phase is about reflecting on your thoughts. Again, it's not about resolving the issue or getting down to the details. Think high level, way above the details to activate an unfocused state of mind with the power of regions in the right hemisphere. Ideas can emerge freely here. Do not discard anything. There is a time for constructive criticism, but not now.

Insight

This phase is fascinating. A burst of gamma band waves hit the brain with the fastest brain waves you can get. Neurons are firing in union back and forth. It's a brief moment with an energetic punch. This is the "A-HA" moment.

Action

This is your chance to harness the energy and creative burst from the Insight phase. It's powerful but short-lived. You must grab the moment and make it happen! Try this the next time you need to brainstorm!

Okay, But You're Not a Creative Person. Now What?

Relax! You are *super*-creative! Every day! Guess what? Every single night when you dream, you are the most creative person in the world! Doesn't it surprise you sometimes what crazy things you dream up? The connections between two things were so crystal clear in your dream, yet when you wake up, it does not make any sense. The reality is that most of the time, you just don't remember come morning.

Apparently, one of the strange traits of creative people is that they believe they are creative. They have the confidence that they can come up with new and exciting ideas. On the other hand, once someone makes them question their own creativity, it's weakened. Once you're under time pressure, for example, the natural reaction is to force creativity. And forcing creativity most likely leads to frustration. Creativity doesn't happen in a vacuum. It brings along lots of stupid ideas. Think of it as a stream, constantly running, not a tap you open and close when you want.

Innovation, the execution and implementation of creativity at the workplace, is top priority nowadays. We hear lots and lots about innovation. There are even people with serious titles driving innovation at work. Doing it right, by treating creativity and innovation as a stream, constantly turning up ideas (good or bad), is the way to go. In a workplace where failure is not an option, creativity and innovation will not likely lead to any breakthrough.

MENTAL TRAVEL: Silva Mind Control, 1994 (Where creative dreams happen.)

It is in my college years that I participate in a Silva Mind Control workshop. It is basically a form of practical meditation, deep reflection, where you reach the same alpha brain waves as in your sleep. Anyway, part of it is about creativity and dreams. After the first day, I decide to keep a dream journal. That night, I wake up and scribble down my dream on a piece of paper, half asleep. It's one of those dreams that you know has something about it, but you can't pinpoint what.

The next morning I looked at my horrible handwriting. Now, the act of scribbling anything down apparently improves dream recall tremendously. So, my dream was very simple and clear:

"I'm sitting in a train, next to me two girls. They are reading the same book. They are French."

And that's it. That was the dream. No significance. Nothing like winning lottery numbers. Yet, when I woke up from that dream, the overall feeling about the significance was so overwhelming that it compelled me to write down those words.

Off I go to the second day of the workshop. Every hour, we have a break, and the rule is to sit somewhere else (NEW PERSPECTIVE?) I kind of forget about my dream. After the last break, I sit down, check my notes and stuff. And I look left.

Two girls are sitting next to me with their books. They are glued to the books. Same book!! They notice my stare. I ask them what they are reading. They say they're high school students and there's a French exam coming up.

I'm floored. I have to explain that I'm not a weirdo, and if it wouldn't have sounded like I was a creep luring girls into his dorm room, I would have shown them the piece of paper on my table. I had several similar dream encounters over the years.

Homework

Now, you can obviously come up with explanations, like I subconsciously was looking for two girls to be able to sit next all day with the hope that they would magically read the same book in French. I might have observed them doing that the day before, who knows? Maybe. My intention is not to convince anyone or sell anything, but to inspire you to try it on your own:

Start a dream journal. Scribble things down right before you wake up, or in the middle of the night. Whatever you remember. The point is to scribble something. Your brain will probably tell you to do later. Don't give in. That's the Red King. You will forget it by then, I guarantee. Do this every day. Every single day. For thirty days.

You will notice three things:

a) You will remember your dreams more often, and in greater detail. It's like telling your brain that you're paying attention now.

b) You will recognize patterns in your dream. Some dream themes are recurring. Days may go by without coming up again but you'll see it in the journal. If your brain wants to tell you something, it will. More and more aggressively. If you don't listen, it will raise its voice. That's how you end up with nightmares, you just won't listen to the subtle warnings.

c) You will see the world in a different way in your awakened state.

Lucid Dreaming

And, of course, if you want to take this to the next level, try Lucid Dreaming. Lucid Dreaming is the ability to realize in your dream that you're dreaming, while maintaining the dream itself. At that point, you experience freedom. Freedom to do anything you want. It's like being in the world's best VR (virtual reality) simulator. My favorite things are flying and going through walls. Again, this is not a dream that just happens to you. You know exactly who you are, you know you're in your bed, you remember your past just as if you were awake. At the same time, you have control over dream world around you.

You can open a door and imagine there's beach. And there it is. A beach. You can imagine a person in the next room and there it is. Lifelike. You can even go back in time and meet a younger you. There are no limits. That is the ultimate creativity! And you know the best part? The next morning, when you wake up, you will clearly remember all of this. Imagine the limitless creativity, engagement, and motivation you have in your power: you can prototype anything in the WORL&D. Just go with the flow!

Before you get too excited, there's a caveat. The Red King will try everything to stop you and throw you out from the flow. How? If you get too excited, you wake up. If you get distracted, you fall back into normal a dream state. To keep your head in the flow, you must not get too excited nor too bored. There's one common trick the Red King pulls when everything fails: false awakening. He makes you believe that you are now awake and your dream is over. Lucid Dreaming is the cream of CREAMs. Oh, and did I mention the price? CREAM is free.

Creative Creek: The Flow

Meanwhile, the flow of the creek takes the boat into a dangerous territory. There's barely room in the underground tunnel to slip through. The Pawns duck. LI DOE follows their lead. He can feel the cave right above his head as they pass under the tight space. Finally, after a short free fall, they're heading toward something that looks like the light at the end of the tunnel. The flow speeds up. They hear a constant rumbling as they're get closer and closer to the light.

Creative Cave: Going with the Flow

LI DOE grabs the boat with one hand, while holding on to the shield as they approach the light.

"This might just be a bad dream. But if not, it's good that we're not inside a mountain."

Then he realizes what he just did.

Oops.

The boat flies out from the "cave" and into the air. They're not in a cave anymore. They're flying from a mountain, heading down a waterfall into a river. The boat lands at the bottom of the waterfall. They all go under as the boat breaks into million pieces. LI DOE keeps hold of his shield, even under water. He notices a familiar figure swimming toward him, also underwater: SHELSTÖDISBORG, the shark.

MENTAL TRAVEL: IKEA, 2010ish
(Where I put together SHELSTÖDISBORG.)

Here's the scenario: you've just purchased the IKEA shelf of your dreams: SHELSTÖDISBORG. It comes in a large box. Ignoring the subtle picture of a crossed-out knife, you slash the box open to spot the colorful, augmented, reality-boosted 3-D pamphlet also known as the instruction booklet. Yeah. You know what I'm talking about. That black-and-white first-grade doodle thing.

Choose Your First Move:

A) You look at the first page of the instructions, and meticulously identify the various parts, nuts, and bolts in the box. Also, you check what tools you need for the job. You might even determine whether you have enough space to work.

B) You ignore the first page with all the nuts and bolts and stuff, and flip through the instructions to get an overall idea of how much wine or beer you need for the job. And THEN you go straight to Step 1.

C) You ignore the first page with all the nuts and bolts and stuff and jump to Step 1. Let's make this happen!

D) You call IKEA for help, as is indicated on page 1.

Result:

A) It drives you insane when people jump into building before they even have a plan. What if they don't have all the parts? What if some nuts and bolts missing? What if the parts are so similar that you can easily mistake them for each other and halfway through the project you realize you need to take it apart and rebuild it? B, C, and D people are nuts!

B) You just need the big picture. Is this the one I ordered? I mean, they all have weird names, right? Got the idea of the whole process. Time to jump in and build. I've been there, done that. I just need some liquid motivation to help. Why would I bother sorting out all nuts and bolts first? I'll get them when I use them. I want to see progress.

C) Oh, please? What can go wrong? It's a twist-left and twist-right thing. Let's live dangerously! Does it ever happen that the shelf is built upside down? Sure! I'll take it apart and rebuild it. But most of the time, it doesn't. So, I save all the up-front worrying and get the job done.

D) I've never in my life met anyone who called IKEA for help. You are truly exceptional.

Types A, B, C and D

Imagine you design a gamified, interactive learning experience. You carefully lay out the rules so people won't get frustrated. You lead them gradually into the core loop," so you can explain the nut and bolts of all tricks ...

You see where I'm going? What you think makes sense may turn others away. Give people options! You're going to have IKEA A, B, C, *and* D people taking your course. Some want ground rules first. Some get bored on page 1. Some need more hand-holding. Some need challenge and constant feedback.

Don't assume that the traditional Nine Shades of Gagne is the golden path for all learners to get excited about your course. Give them options! However, if something is absolutely crucial for the success of the gamified solution, make it mandatory. Be quick. Be creative. Make them walk through as a training to get their badge to roam free. Most people would skip demos and get frustrated with the gameplay.

If you're working on a team, remember there's no right or wrong way. We're wired differently. Balance the intrinsic and extrinsic rewards to maintain a healthy, scalable experience for all.

Speaking of Rewards

Rewards should be a no-brainer. You perform, you get rewarded. The more reward you're promised, the more motivated you are to perform. Win-win.

Of course, it doesn't actually work like that. You are probably familiar with Daniel Pink's *Drive: The Surprising Truth About What Motivates Us* and Andrzej Marczewski's work on balancing rewards against effort in gamification.[8] If not, I strongly suggest researching them.

How About Gamification of Learning?

True story: a couple of years ago a prominent learning platform vendor came to us to promote—you guessed it!—their platform. To gain support, a handpicked group of people were given a chance to create a sample course on the platform. This is where the rewards come in. It was decided that the "best" course would win an iPad.

Of course I jumped in to showcase my skills, both as an instructional designer and developer. Honestly, the iPad sounded good, but for me, it was more about the challenge, the challenge to show how quickly I could create an engaging and effective course.

"Give me three days and a sandbox" is my attitude towards any technology platform. After a couple of days, I concluded that the user experience on the platform at that time was not something that I would recommend to others. I dropped out of the challenge.

Who won the iPad? Funny, you ask. Apparently, nobody won after the "first round." It was decided (after the fact) that participants needed to do more rounds to win. Eventually, someone did, but by then, it was clear the implementation of this platform would not be successful. And let's be clear, there's nothing more demotivating than changing the game rules midway.

Have you had any learning challenges where external monetary reward was offered as motivation? How did that turn out? Be careful with external motivation only! In the long run, it might backfire, and you will

8   Andrzej Marczewski. *Even Ninja Monkeys Like to Play: Gamification, Game Thinking, and Motivational Design* (2015); see pages 65-80.

alienate many who have no chance to win. Scalability is also crucial. Are you giving out iPads every time? After a while your extrinsic motivators may turn into meaningless points, badges, and leaderboard positions for most you actually wanted to motivate.

Speaking of Motivation!

How motivated are you when you hear the word "training"? How about when you visualize it as the moving checkbox for every event on a giant MS Project, right in-between where everything else can go wrong and the frozen, drop-dead deadline? Not so much?

How do you measure the success of training? Are any of these measurements familiar?

1) Number of completions.
2) Time learner spent in the course.
3) How much learner claims to have enjoyed the course.
4) Number of times learner relaunched the course.
5) The average smilesheet rate (Level 1).
6) Passing rate (five questions at the end of the course).

Let's say a manager doesn't know who took the training and who did not. Would they see significant difference between work performances? If not, would you say the training was a waste of money?

One of the biggest issues HR deals with is employee engagement. Losing top talent is costly. Part of employee engagement is the ability to grow at the workplace, and growing skills is what L&D is all about. Then why are learners not engaged and motivated at work?

Learner Engagement

If you're in charge of learner engagement and motivation, you're probably looking at a new Learning Management System, gamification, microlearning, mobile learning, AR/VR, and other hot trends as an answer to your excellent question: Why are learners not engaged and motivated to learn at work?

Before you invest time and resources in new technology, let's take a step back and revisit engagement and motivation! (For more on why motivation doesn't work, check out Susan Fowler's *Why Motivating People Doesn't Work ... and What Does*).

People spend significant amounts of informal learning time on YouTube, social media, forums; they're asking peers constantly for answers. They are engaged and motivated. So, the question isn't why are they not engaged and motivated at work, but how can you engage and motivate them to learn. You can motivate them with engaging content, right? To develop their talent, right?

"I'm a human resource, develop me!" said no one ever full of engagement and motivation. On the other hand, employees *do* want to grow and learn when challenged at work.

Retaining Talented Humans!

What if our job was to help them develop, rather than developing them? To show relevance to their goals, instead of highlighting measurable learning objectives? To facilitate connections, shared knowledge, in the workplace ecosystem, rather than locking vital information in courses? Are we doing a good job retaining talent that way?

Josh Bersin, author of *The Blended Learning Book,* says, "Not really."

"We can't 'retain' people, we can only 'attract them.' We can't 'engage them' but we can 'inspire and support them.' We can't only 'train them' but we can 'enable them to learn' and 'give them the opportunities to develop.'"[9]

Bersin's article explores the mindset shift from retaining, developing, and training "human resources" to providing them with engaging opportunities to grow. So, let's keep humans in mind! How do you translate all this into some practical example for humans, like designing an eLearning course? (Assuming you actually need an eLearning course, based on Cathy Moore's action mapping.)

---

9   https://www.forbes.com/sites/joshbersin/2014/04/10/its-time-to-rethink-the-employee-engagement-issue/#78defe6b6cf3

Learner Engagement for Humans: Five Design Steps

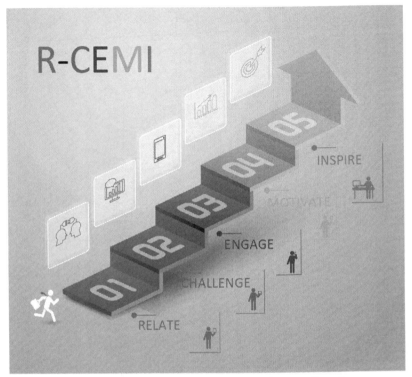

Relate - Challenge - Engage - Motivate - Inspire

Step 0: Grab Attention!

If you ask people about their last eLearning experience, what words will you hear from them? That human (resource) who's about to take a course has a workload, a demanding boss, hectic work environment, crazy deadlines, an ongoing life. Life before, during, and after your course. That human is only a learner for ten to fifteen minutes, while human for a life. Therefore, you must show the relevance to each phase. Focusing on only the "learning" (during) reduces your chances of engaging them.

Tip: Attention grabbing may happen even before the learning event. How about an email with a short scenario? Learners will find the answer in the course.

Step 1: Relate

Most of the time, however, the Step 0 (Grab Attention!) can't happen before the learning event. In that case, you must integrate it with Step 1 (Relate).

"Content is King!" says the old wisdom. Not anymore! Context is King and Action is Queen! Give humans clear answers to their two fundamental questions:

How does this course relate to me?

What do you want me to do differently after this course?

Remember, you must show the relevance to each phase of human life, not only the "learning" (during). Humans may pass a course with flying colors but with no intention or knowledge of how and when to apply it after. If you're merely measuring completion and seat time, this is good news. You're done. If you're focusing on actual business goals, read on!

This is where Instructional Designers usually bring up my favorite discussion topic of the learning experience: learning objectives.

Have you ever tried a bottle of Smartwater? It's tasty, measurable and arguably far more clever than regular water. But that's not the only way to deal with thirst.

So, let me ask you this: What's the primary goal of your learning objectives?

a) Prime learning, as in guide the learner's focus? (Research shows it *does* help.)

b) Engage learners to take the actual course, so you can count on completion data?

c) Motivate learners to apply knowledge or skill to grow?

There's no good or bad answer here, but you must be clear about your goal when designing the experience. Learning objectives on the first page may not be the only way (to attempt) to grab their attention and show relevance.

Tip: Show them a realistic scenario. Give them a question to ponder, such as consequences of actions at the company due to lack of knowledge or skill.

Step 2: Challenge

Humans engage when they're challenged to use their brain, not when they're asked to move their mouse.

You can probably hear your Subject Matter Experts' and stakeholders' voices in your head: "Challenges can be frustrating! What if they don't know the answer? You wouldn't want them to fail, would you?"

Tip: Here's a suggestion to avoid frustration. Provide a basic challenge in a well-defined context. Give them the option for a hint. If they don't use the hint but select the right answer, acknowledge their achievement, and add some complexity to the challenge. Tell humans they will find the correct answer by the end of the module. You've just created an open loop!

Step 3: Engage

The human brain is wired to close open loops (like cliff-hangers). Humans want to know the answer to the more complex scenario you presented previously; use that innate desire to keep them engaged. Show their progress, keep them challenged, all the while scaffolding their experience with a positive feedback loop. Don't throw them under the bus, but, rather, put them in the driver's seat with adequate support. Michael Allen has more details on how to implement CCAF (Context, Challenge, Activity, Feedback) in his book *Insert book title here*. Think of it as loops within the overall progress. I like to visualize them as a cone spiral, as every loop builds on the previous one, getting wide and more and more challenging.

Tip: Feedback (and reflection on the feedback) is where learning happens. "Incorrect" and "Great Job!" don't add value; they just burn the working memory. Feedback doesn't always have to be text either. Games have mastered feedback as a primary tool of engagement. Read more on Karl Kapp's blog, "insert name of blog," about feedback used as a game element.

Step 4: Motivate

So far, we've addressed the before and during human stages. You probably know that a learning event and its content will be forgotten (google the Ebbinghaus forgetting curve) soon if not reinforced after the event. But did you know that Ebbinghaus came up with his forgetting equation based on memorizing nonsense syllables? How often do you need to recall nonsense syllables at work? Benedict Carey argues in *How We Learn* that forgetting is not simply the decay of human memory but a filter powering the mind to enable and deepen learning itself.[10] While you have control over engagement during a learning experience, you probably have much less to say about what happens to the humans after. Therefore, you need to design the learning experience to motivate humans to apply their knowledge or skill. But how?

Tip: Do not design the experience for yourself! What motivates you may not motivate others.

Motivation is an illogical beast! The challenge you're facing is that humans are not motivated by the same things. Some like competing, some like social interactions, others prefer certificates to show their progress. Game thinking, the practical application of engagement and motivation, may help you become more effective in that motivation space. Approaches such as Andrzej Marczewski's RAMP (Relatedness, Autonomy, Mastery, and Purpose) or Keller's ARCS model (Attention, Relevance, Confidence, Satisfaction) are good places to start digging for additional gun powder to attack this beast.

A few practical motivational takeaways:

1) Don't rely on extrinsic motivation only (rewards, money, prize). They may boost initial motivation but often backfire in the long run.

---

10   Benedict Carey. *How We Learn: The Surprising Truth About When, Where, and Why It Happens* (Kindle edition, 2014).

2) If you don't know Julie Dirksen, stop reading this! Read her *Design for How People Learn* first, especially, the chapter about, surprise, motivation! Per Susan Fowler, motivation is a skill. Humans can learn to choose and create optimal motivational experiences for themselves driven intrinsically by the self-determination theory (autonomy, relatedness, and competence).

3) Is there a social platform available? Give learners a challenge to share how they used their skills within a week.

4) Have learners type/write down how they're going to apply the knowledge. Maybe think of a person they want to share this knowledge with? Any workplace anchors that will trigger motivation can help them remember.

5) If you don't have any time to read research or books, at least check out Daniel Pink's TED talk.

The goal is to provide different avenues for humans to find their own intrinsic motivation, rather than motivating them get somewhere directly. It's not just about where they want to be; it's as much as about why and how they get there.

Step 5: Inspire

In the long run, humans are measured on their performance at work. A short-term motivation may reinforce the application of learning, but it's rare that you can "teach" everything humans need to be able to do within the learning experience. Therefore, you must design the experience to inspire them to learn more, use resources, be social, work out loud ("show their work").

Tip: Use the whole workplace ecosystem (formal and informal learning tools and platforms) available for humans to grow to inspire them to do more than they thought they ever could.

Motivation Conclusion

Ultimately, it's not just the points, badges, or even money that will engage and retain talents. It's the intrinsic motivation from the combination of ARCS (Attention, Relevance, Confidence, Satisfaction) and RAMP (Relatedness, Autonomy, Mastery, and Purpose). Remember these five steps next time when designing a learning experience for humans!

Tip: You don't have to do this alone! Connect with others on social media (here's how and why), work out loud! Share best practices and worst failures! At the end of the day, we are all humans.

MENTAL TIME TRAVEL: Teaching Practicum, 1998 (In which I invoke Run-D.M.C.)

Imagine the time before search engines. Before YouTube, Facebook, and Google. People would buy CDs and tapes to listen to their favorite bands. This is around the time that I am about to graduate from college with a degree in English. In order to graduate, I have to complete two teaching practicums. One in an elementary school, the other in a high school. The elementary school practicum goes well. They love my creativity and enthusiasm. So much so that after twenty-five years one of those students finds me on Facebook to tell me how my teaching influenced him to become an English major. I actually made a difference in someone's life? Scary.

But this story is about my teaching experience at the high school. And, more specifically, about motivation.

A colleague and I are handpicked to go to this disaster of a high school to teach English with no "friendly" support. I'm not exaggerating. The school is rumored to be closed soon. Teachers are trying to figure out where to go, students couldn't care less.

Day 1 of Hell

We learn two important facts on day 1.

1. Teachers go to class as late as they can, and leave as soon as they can.

2. The English teacher (who we are subbing for) has been on "medical leave" for two months, which might have something to do with the class behavior. (This truth also makes it clear that technically speaking, English classes have been "free time" for the class for months.)

We also get good tips from teachers, such as don't turn your back to the class because that's when they typically throw things. Real things, not imaginary things.

Week 1 of Hell

By the end of week 1, I decide that I will not pursue a teaching career. I have about thirty kids in a class (a huge number in Hungary). About four have clear motivation to learn something, twenty-seven are neutral, and three are ... ABSOLUTE HELL!! Those three sit in the back causing trouble. I nickname them the Three Terrible Troublemakers (T3). The T3 pretend to be the local hip-hop gang. One of them has blue hair. Not that I would discriminate based on color, but it was pretty obvious that they have no intention of paying attention to anything. They were there to rap.

Week 2 of Hell

By week 2, it is clear that just sheer survival will require some kind of truce with the T3. So, after a painful class, I pull them aside and engage them in what we call today a "managing difficult conversations" session. I want to find out what motivates them enough to make a compromise.

I guess nobody ever asked them this question before, because they are stunned at first. After some hesitation, they all agree that the hip-hop (or is it rap?) music they listen to is the best thing ever, and that class interferes with their favorite activity, rapping (or is it hip-hopping?).

I offer to build the next English class around their favorite hip-hop song, as long as they hip-hop cooperate. They give me the title and the name of the band. When I ask them what the song is about, they scream/rap/hip it and hop it, somewhat. It is obvious they have no idea what they are "rapping."

Hell's Turning Point

Well, the song is "It's Like That!" by Run-D.M.C. Bring back any memories? Here's how things unfold.

I enter the class, and there is silence. There's no raucous, no screaming, no running, no rapping around. The T3 are sitting in the front row, equipped with pencils, paper, and a huge boombox (this is way before iPods) ready to roll, or rather, ready to rap.

On that day the T3 learn the lesson of their life. If there had been a learning objective written on their face, it would have been something like: "By the end of this lesson, learners will be able to understand what the heck they are rapping."

And the relevant lyrics from the song go like this:

"You should have gone to school, you could've learned a trade
But you laid in the bed where the bums have laid
Now all the time you're crying that you're underpaid
It's like that (what?) and that's the way it is
Huh!

One thing I know is that life is short
So listen up homeboy, give this a thought
The next time someone's teaching why don't you get taught?
It's like that (what?) and that's the way it is."

The expression on their faces is priceless. Like (SPOILER ALERT!!) learning that Santa is not real. Interestingly enough, the T3 would never bother the class anymore. They also stop listening to Run-D.M.C. It's like that (what?)! And that's the way it is with motivation. Motivation is a personal relationship.

Motivation in learning projects? Stakeholder, manager, SME say the humans are still not motivated? They are. They're just not motivated by what's in front of them. One of the biggest risk when designing any learning solutions is not knowing your target audience. Relying on the SME's and stakeholder's description only may lead to surprising results.

The Biggest Risk

I asked Clark Quinn and Julie Dirksen to tell me something they wish they had been told when they first started working. By coincidence (or not), both emphasized the importance of knowing your audience!

Clark Quinn

"Don't ever underestimate the power of real users in the design process (e.g., not trusting what SMEs tell you). We were asked to develop a game to help kids who grow up without parents (e.g., foster care, orphanages) learn to cope on their own. The counselors told us that the kids needed to learn to shop and cook. Yes, well. But the kids told us a different story; what was challenging was the chain of things: you could get money, but you needed to apply, and they wouldn't give it to you, instead you needed a bank account, and to do that you needed ID, … That's what we built, and that was a real success.

"The lesson is that experts can't really tell you what it is they do, and sometimes they're wrong. Find a way to get the real information, triangulate with the users, their managers, or whoever can give you insight."

Julie Dirksen

"Don't ever underestimate the importance of testing your ideas and getting feedback. The best solution is the one that works, and if you don't know what works and what doesn't, it's very hard to improve as a professional. Test prototypes of your ideas, and figure out how to get feedback. Even when it's hard to get large-scale quantitative feedback, small-scale qualitative can give you useful insights. Always talk to your end users."

Zsolt Olah

"Accept feedback as the impression of your work, not the intention of your work. Nothing motivates better than honest, brutal but constructive feedback on your work. In theory. In practice, it hurts. I participated once in a writing group, where we sat in a room to discuss each other's work. The author was "dead." No defense, no explanation, no comments. During the discussion, the author was not allowed to react. The process teaches you to accept feedback as the impression of your work, not the intention of your work.

"When you receive feedback on your storyboard or eLearning prototype, remember, what counts is the impression, not what you intended to do. Reviewers don't see what's in your head. They can only see what's on the paper. When humans are taking your course, there's no room for explanations or defense. You're suffering from the curse of knowledge. You've seen the content navigation a hundred times. End users will see it only once!"

MENTAL TRAVEL: Hungary, 1990s
(Where I play songs on a Russian vacuum cleaner.)

When you're a teenager, you don't really question whether you should stay or you should go. And by that, I mean whether you should continue doing something just because it's fun even if you're not really good at it. You do what you feel like, emotions and relationships drive most of our decisions. As we grow up, we tend to do things that either make money or we're good at because we don't want to waste our precious free time on failures.

In high school, I had the nickname "Maestro." Yes, I know it sounds ridiculous. It actually had something to do with learning. (When I worked for the Peace Corps in Hungary, the U.S. corporate leadership immediately thought of the *Seinfeld* episode, and wanted me to never bring up my nickname.[11])

This is the same time I decide to become a famous musician. (Note, not just any musician, but a famous musician!) We have an old Russian keyboard at home. Nope, not an electronic one. One that sounds like a vacuum cleaner as its motor pumps air through the keys. I spend the entire summer, eight hours a day, working on separating my left and right hands. I mean, they are already separate, but I just can't play different things with the left and right at the same time. It's not as easy as it sounds! Especially on a Russian vacuum cleaner. But ... by the end of the summer, I learn the basics of playing on a vacuum cleaner.

And this achievement leads to the obvious: let's create a band. A band we call Imitater Kongs. Don't even ask! With a band comes some challenges. Someone needs to write songs! Somehow it lands on me. Never in my life has anyone told me how to write a song. And that was before the internet, so you can't even search for kitty cats online, much less songwriting.

Interestingly, nobody in our group is really good at singing, which is why we have three people singing at once (we figure there's a bigger chance of hitting the right key if we triple them). If you want to learn more about me, here's a gameful interactive video course I made in Articulate Storyline. Best I can describe the experience is as an HR-appropriate strip-rock-paper-scissors interactive video interview. (It was featured at DevLearn in 2015.)[12]

Back to my original point: was I really good at playing the keyboard and writing songs? No, I was horrible. But it was fun. And the weirdest thing? People who had been learning instruments for years asking me how I came up with songs. They could actually play. They could actually read sheet music. They could even sing. But they could not come up with a song. Mystery. And that's how I got the nickname Maestro.

Tip: Have fun! Make something! Earn a nickname!

---

11   https://en.wikipedia.org/wiki/The_Maestro_(Seinfeld)

12   https://www.rabbitoreg.com/2015/09/06/
video-interview-with-zsolt-olah-hr-appropriate-strip-rock-paper-scissors-style/.

And while you're doing all of the above, avoid comparing yourself to the top of the chart. When you create something new, it doesn't matter how bad it is. You know why? Because the worst thing you've ever created is still much better than the most perfect one you never tried. Go, and create something! Use a new tool! An instrument! Code! Make a game! Write a blog! Start your YouTube channel! Snapchat! Whatever! Have fun!

There are days when I think this book is the stupidest idea I've ever had. Why? Because stupid ideas always seem fun in the beginning, then they always turn into a lot of work somehow! The only way to get the work done is you're motivated. But that's easier said than done.

A Motivation, a To-Do List, and a Chemical Called Dopamine Walk into a Brain …

I captured my thoughts on the Games and Gamification Online Summit in 2016 with Squigl. Squigl from TruScribe is whiteboard animation tool to get message across EXTREMELY FAST. Capturing thoughts at the end of the summit doesn't need days of sophisticated work to spread the message.

The reason I brought this piece of memory back is simple. The glyphs you see in Squigl clips are not random doodles. They serve two main purposes: motion and meaning.

Our brain is wired to pay attention to motion. That's why all those pesky ads are moving on the screen all the time. On of the reasons why they're effective is all about dopamine. Dopamine is a chemical your brain releases when you run a marathon, win a game, capture a Pokémon. But his accomplishments don't have to be physical. Remembering where your keys are, making a decision, etc., are all accomplishments, hence they trigger dopamine.

Recognizing patterns is another accomplishment. In whiteboard videos, a hand is drawing something. Your brain pays attention to the motion, trying hard to figure out the pattern. Remember, the brain doesn't like open loops. The moment the drawing is complete in your head, you feel a sense of accomplishment. Then, suddenly, another dose of excitement comes: making the association between the drawing and the meaning in the context of the clip. Dopamine again.

That's why it's crucial to support your words by images that highlight the meaning, not just the words themselves.

Here's an example: in my recap, I used a glyph for Pinocchio, whose nose gets bigger with every lie. When you see the hand drawing the character, your brain recognizes the pattern (based on cultural filters). Accomplishment! Then, it realizes the meaning behind the drawing and the words:

"As Shakira says, hips and numbers don't **lie**."

Accomplishments! It feel good! Even if the accomplishment consists of making a choice to cancel a dreaded meeting, to postpone a workout because it's raining, or to decide not to write that first paragraph! Love it! It feels good not to do something. It does! You feel relieved! Easiest way to boost your dopamine level is to put a bunch of commitments on your to-do list, and then cancel them when they're due.

What's on Your To-Do List?

We've all heard the advantages of using to-do lists. You probably use them daily. But are you harnessing the real power of a to-do list? What's your VERY FIRST ITEM?

"Write a to-do list"? DONE! Check! Already feeling good about ourselves, yeah! Every single checkmark is like a sugar high! We feel accomplished and motivated (somewhat) to do the next task. And when all done? Time for celebration! Cake by the Ocean!

Well, It's All Your Head!

Thing is, it's all your head! Really! Thanks to dopamine. Now, for a long time I thought dopamine was just a pleasure drug, the happy dose I get when I finish a task, run a marathon, write a screenplay, or catch a Pokémon. After doing some research, I found new appreciation for dopamine and the complexity of its function. [13]

Is It All About Pleasure?

The article mentions how dopamine levels rise in soldiers with PTSD when they hear gunfire. That's not pleasure! This makes me think of dopamine differently, as pertains to dealing with motivation in the workplace learning. Gamification uses motivation as its underlying principle. Pleasure is a great motivator, so naturally I want to get to the bottom of

---

[13]   http://blog.idonethis.com/the-science-of-motivation-your-brain-on-dopamine/

what's happening with dopamine. If dopamine isn't about pleasure only, then what? And how can I leverage that when designing learning activities or applying game thinking?

According to the article, the true purpose of dopamine might be motivation RIGHT BEFORE the reward, either motivating us to DO SOMETHING to gain the reward (pleasure) or to AVOID DANGER (like in the case of the solders with PTSD).

Maybe that's why to-do lists are crucial. You break large tasks into smaller, distinct steps to get motivated by each completion. And while you're enjoying the pleasurable moment of checking one off, you're motivated to move on to the next, to repeat the pleasure. The higher your dopamine level, the more motivated you are to work hard on the next challenge! Got it.

"Low levels of dopamine make people and other animals less likely to work for things, so it has more to do with motivation and cost/benefit analyses than pleasure itself."

Okay, so it's about the dopamine level. If that's the case, can we boost dopamine level at the workplace? How about training? If learners' motivation relies on their dopamine level, is there anything we can do to boost it? HR-appropriately, of course.

Not So Simple

After more research, the answer got a little more complicated. Another study showed that both "slackers" and "go-getters" in a group had dopamine present, yet their actions were completely opposite. Now what? Is it not the dopamine level itself that determines our motivation to achieve?

What-If Moment

And that brings me to my a-ha moment. Actually, it's more like a what-if moment. What if we are actually given a choice? What if we choose the path to walk, and from there on, dopamine drives us? What if we must take that first step? What if our brain is wired to support, but it takes our lead on where to go? That first step is our choice.

What's the Moral of the Story for Learning?

Do not assume that writing up five learning objectives will catapult learners into the path of dopamine pleasure. Even if there's a WIIF in each, they're looking at the number of slides: 60???

Help learners make that first choice! Help them choose the path! Give them a small task that requires some effort but not enough to be a hurdle. It's like starting a to-do list with "write a to-do list."

Do not isolate learners in an LMS bubble where it's them vs. the machine. A workplace is a social venue. If it's an eLearning course, find a role model, someone who has the knowledge and skills the course is about. Have them do a thirty-second testimony at the beginning of the course: this is what I learned from this course, and this is how it made my life easier. Done. Watch what happens!

Give positive, constructive feedback frequently. Show them the to-do list. Show their progress! Make them think, and have them make meaningful decisions with consequences, followed by constructive feedback.

So, next time you create a to-do list, you know how to start it! And cross that first item off right after you're done writing the list! Done. You just experienced the drug of pleasure, dopamine.

Under the Bridge

LI DOE opens his eyes. A wolf howls in the distance. LI DOE is on the ground, right next to a blue river. Above him is a bridge. What happened in the Creative Cave seems like just a bad dream. Someone's long shadow covers LI DOE's Magic Mojo Hexad. The Sun doesn't even get down here, so LI DOE is somewhat confused about the shadow. The shadow belongs to a tall man, wearing a red robe and dark sunglasses.

LI DOE: "Where am I?"

Red King: "A Queen under the lone sky. Welcome to downtown! Welcome to my town, among the red hot shadows of the WORL&D."

LI DOE: "Who are you?"

The Red King leans over LI DOE. Uncomfortably close. LI DOE can see his own reflection in the Red King's dark sunglasses.

Red King: "Look into my eyes! You see them? That's where my demons hide."

The Red King pulls a chili pepper out of his pocket and bites into the hot beast.

Red King: "Some call me Captain Saicin. You know why? Capsaicin is a chemical that stimulates the neural sensors in the tongue and skin. They also detect rising temperatures. Your neurons are literally telling the brain: your mouth is on FIRE. With that, adrenaline flows and the heart pumps faster. And you feel good, my friend! But it's all in your head. It's all in your head. There's no fire, there's no pain."

The Red King throws away the rest the chili pepper and snaps with his fingers. LI DOE has no idea what that means, but he has a sinister feeling. A slight breeze hits LI DOE's face. He jumps up from the ground. Above the Red King's head, the infamous Scythe flies under the bridge. The Red King kicks the Magic Mojo Hexad to LI DOE.

Red King: "You failed, my friend. You have not completed the Creative Cave mission. The moment you questioned your creativity inside, you failed. Like many others before you."

The Red King snaps his fingers again and the Scythe strikes. It scratches LI DOE's hand, just enough to hurt.

Red King: "This is just a warning. Go home, my friend! Go home before it's too late. Don't get too close to the dark."

The Red King points at his dark sunglasses.

LI DOE: "I know who you are!"

The Red King smirks and disappears with the Scythe in a wink. LI DOE picks up the shield. The CREAM traits are turned on. A White Bishop's head pops up from the bridge above.

White Bishop: "Check, my flatmate! You need a spade if you want to dig a hole!"

LI DOE: "I don't understand. I thought the Red King said I failed."

White Bishop: "Failure depends how you define and measure success, my flatmate. The Red King measures in completions. We measure in change of behavior. At the core, we are about humans. The Red King is about numbers. C'mon up here. This is the Amyg D'la Bridge. Emotions can be dangerously high around here."

LI DOE: "A Queen under the lone sky? What does that mean?"

LI DOE angrily stamps on the chili pepper on the ground, over and over again until it's unrecognizable. Suddenly he stops. He spins around to see a White Bunny staring at him. The White Bunny runs away scared to death.

LI DOE: "Hey, I didn't mean to."

IRL CHALLENGES:

1. Find a problem that requires a creative solution.

2. Immerse yourself in research about the problem. Read and discuss as much as you can. Don't solution, just let it stew! Do something else, focus on something completely different.

3. Sleep on the problem if you can.

4. Sit down, and brainstorm solutions for fifteen minutes. Do not lift your pen! Just write whatever comes to your mind. Do not discard your thoughts, just write them down.

Chapter Four

HUMAN-CENTERED DESIGN
(FROM CONTENT TO CONTEXT)

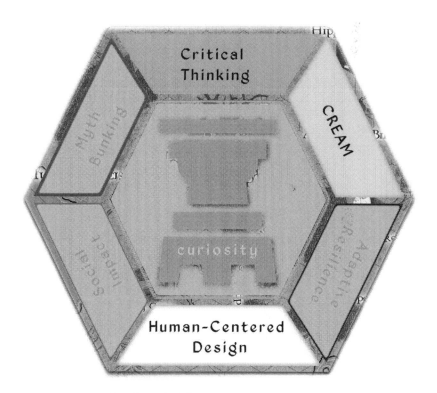

Pursuit of Trait 3/6: Human-Centered Design

Where Are We?

The origins of the Amyg D'la Bridge are unknown. The almond-shaped set of neurons-bricks located deep inside the island's medial temporal lobe serves the purpose of controlling emotions. Legend says that as you go across the bridge to the Hippo Campus, you either feel fear, anger, or pleasure, depending on what's on your mind. Either way, it's an emotional journey. On those snowy winter days when the bridge is closed, residents go nuts, as if they've lost their sense of fear completely. You see them walking on fire, jumping into the ice-cold ocean, even designing eLearning without a list of learning objectives on the first slide

As LI DOE stands on the bridge, looking down at the blue river, the White Bishop constantly hops around.

White Bishop: "Check, my flatmate! You need a spade if you want to dig a hole!"

LI DOE: "How come we skipped the Adaptive Resilience?"

White Bishop: "Life is not linear. I love zigzagging all around."

LI DOE: "That I can see."

White Bishop: "Checkpoint, my flatmate! Let's play! The more you take away from me, the bigger I get. Who am I?"

LI DOE: "I heard that question before."

White Bishop: "Of course, this is testing your long-term memory. So, who am I?"

LI DOE: "Why did you pick the spade?"

White Bishop: "Is that your answer, flatmate?"

LI DOE: "No, another question from long-term memory I just remembered. I'm afraid I don't know the answer, flatmate."

A strange noise breaks the scene.

LI DOE: "What was that?"

White Bishop: "A beat. My happy heart."

The Bishop grabs LI DOE and zigzags with him to the other side of the bridge, to shed in an open field with gardening tools. The Bishop grabs a spade.

LI DOE's memory churn. Bad memories about movies where victims had to dig their own shallow grave.

White Bishop: "Digging it, flatmate? Digging it? Let's play happy heart! The more you take away from me, the bigger I get. Select one of the following: A) All of the above or B) All of the below."

LI DOE looks at the spade and the hole the Bishop made and bursts out laughing for no reason.

LI DOE: "This happy heart test doesn't make any sense. It's a hole, no matter how you look at it."

White Bishop: "Correct! A hole! The more you take away from me, the bigger I get. Just like your curiosity muscle. The more you use it, the stronger it gets. Come with me, flatmate! I'll show you something you're going to love."

The Bishop hops away.

LI DOE: "I can't hop, remember, flatmate?"

Once you cross the Amyg D'la Bridge and get closer to Hippo Campus, the long-term storage area owned by the Sea H'orce family, the scenery turns beautiful. The Sea H'orce family was one of the main sponsors behind the SILO. In fact, legend has it, there might be underground connections between the SILO and the Hippo Campus. While the storage place is supposed to be enormous, the Standard Operating Procedures (SOP) of the facility do not allow short-term items to be stored here. Only long-term memories are accepted. This rule is strictly reinforced.

White Bishop: "Welcome to the Hippo Campus, the biggest Mr. Storage ever built! Because Hippo Campus is strongly tied to emotions, its infrastructure follows Human-Centered Design. Let's hop around!"

The Bishop hops and hops until he gets back to his original place. As they haven't moved an inch, LI DOE starts feeling awkward. The landscape is green, lavish. The pond is lovely, the light breeze is perfect for an afternoon picnic. The whole scene is straight out of a children's book.

LI DOE: "I mean, it's pretty here but I don't see building or any design here. How far is it?"

White Bishop: "Oh, it's not a building, flatmate. This is it. It's nature all around. Get off the path, lie down on the grass. Breathe the fresh air. Feel the breeze. That is Human-Centered Design. It's not about getting from point A to point B anymore; it's about you enjoying the ride there."

Human-Centered Design

Human-Centered Design may sound like some lofty corporate flavor-of-the-month initiative. It's not. In the history of L&D, we've often felt that we've found the silver bullet in some emerging technology. For example, the pure joy of the sharable learning object in the Learning Management System brought tears to our eyes in the form of SCORM. With the endless possibilities for Augment Reality, Virtual Reality, 360 videos, microlearning, gamification platforms, we've spent the last decade on prepping for the future of learning.

For a moment, let's stop chasing the future of learning. Let's look at the "now of learning." Let's stop and think for a moment about priorities, about who we are as learning professionals. We're not about technology. We're about humans. Human-Centered Design simply means that we put humans back into the center of our focus when designing solutions. Design Thinking and Game Thinking are both Human-Centered Design approaches to problem-solving, and by problem-solving I don't mean training solutions. Have you ever worked on project where the training was clearly necessary because of bad design? System rollouts with horrible interfaces? Process support tools that create even more confusion? A simplified sales process that has more steps, in the end, than its predecessor? I've had multiple occasions when I used Photoshop to mimic an application screen that wasn't even built yet, but the training had to roll out. At some point, we built a simulation as a training tool that worked better than the actual application (and we had to slow it down to make it real).

Human-Centered Design doesn't start or end with learning. It starts with looking at problems from the user's perspective, rather than from the perspective of the stakeholders, SMEs, legal, or HR. Now, if your job is simply to work with instructions and create training solutions when requested, you may think, given your constraints, that there's nothing useful in this chapter. You're right. There's nothing to see here.

Let's think for a minute about some disruptive companies and their solutions. Whether you like it or not, companies like Amazon, Uber, and Airbnb are changing the world. You may say Uber is killing the cab industry, but the only guilty party is their Human-Centered Design. They managed to solve pain points of the cab experience: no idea where the cab is, drivers talking on the phone, dirty old cop cars, cash only, etc. They replaced those pain points with options humans prefer. It wasn't Uber that killed the cab industry; it was the cabs' own inability to adapt and improve.

Same goes to hotels: expensive, hard-to-find rooms; horrible service; no feedback. Airbnb offered a solution: don't just stay there, live there.

Do you remember retail stores before Amazon? Crowds, no customer service, no returns … With Amazon, you hover over an item and it's being shipped. Literally.

Companies who use Human-Centered Design can find these pain points and offer a better, faster, cheaper user experience.

In a cab, you were treated as a passenger. As a passenger, you paid the cab driver to take you from point A to point B. The trip was purely transactional. As a passenger, you paid to get moved from one place to another. With Uber and Lyft, however, you are treated as a human who happens to need a ride. A conversation between humans takes place, while you happen to be traveling to the same destination. Suddenly, you don't feel like you're being hauled to jail in a cop car. And you're willing to pay for the experience. (I'm not promoting these above-mentioned companies, just pointing out the service they offer.)

What happens when someone comes along and offers a better, faster and cheaper alternative to L&D courses? Are we improving and innovating fast enough to adapt before it's too late? Human-Centered Design is not about talking; it's about changing the focus. It's about actually changing the focus from content to user experience. Building courses for everything is like assuming our cab is doing just fine: a little bit slow, a little bit off the track, a little bit late, but it's been like that for a long time. Careful! Today, it's not just about getting from point A to point B. It's about whether humans enjoy the ride. That's why I'm not a fan of the "learner" approach. When you treat your audience as learners, you're focusing on learning, like the cab driver who doesn't care where you come from or what you're doing after the trip. His job is dealing with a passenger. (I can only speak to workplace learning, where the primary focus of employees is work and not learning. In K12 and higher education, circumstances might be completely different.)

Let's Play a Game!

LI DOE lies on the grass with a lazy Sunday, fresh-cut grass attitude as he looks up to spot a kite flying in the blue sky. LI DOE's algorithm stops churning. There's something peaceful about kites. This is the first time LI DOE's algorithm produces something illogical. LI DOE feels relaxed when, in fact, he knows he should be heading home.

White Bishop: "Let's play games, flatmate!"

LI DOE: "What kinds of games?"

White Bishop: "I like your attitude, dude!"

MENTAL TRAVEL: Heves, Hungary, 1999
(Where World War Two breaks out in my home.)

It is in sixth grade that I win the chess championship at school. I don't really like chess. I always felt it has too many restrictions. I know, every Pawn's dream is to become a Queen. Did you know that there's no limitation on how many Pawns can turn into a Queen? In theory, you could get eight of them running around! The most I've found was in a game played by Emil Szalanczy versus Thi Mai Hung Nguyen (2009). The game had six Queens on the board! If you like logic, chess is your game. What I learned playing chess is that half of winning is not about knowing all the moves, it's about figuring out your opponent. There you go, chess is not only about the pieces and moves on the board, it's about the humans at the table.

If you know me, you know I'm a big proponent of game thinking for learning. I grew up playing games. There was a tradition in our family to buy a different board game every year and play it during the holidays.

Playing cards with friends and extended family equals hours of entertainment. If you've ever played Robber's Rummy with four or five people, you know it's a mind gym. You must be able to play hundreds of moves in your head, while watching others playing, in case they mess up your plan. In college, we would pull all-nighters playing Risk. Speaking of Risk!

Given my family tradition, it seems a natural move to get a board game when my fiancée's family is about to visit us in Hungary for the first time. What risk? I mean, what could possibly go wrong, right? My parents, me and my fiancée, her brother and my would-be in-laws bonding over a board game.

I search on Amazon to get something good and exciting. Based on raving reviews, we land on Axis and Allies. Axis and Allies is a World War Two strategy board game, where multiple countries are killing each other. Perfect for family bonding.

The first hour I spend breaking out all the plastic soldiers, tanks, aircrafts, and you-name-it from the mold. But then the fun begins. We all gather around the table and pick a country. I open the twelve-page booklet, titled "Rules," and start reading it to educate everyone on how to play. Now, there aren't any pictures in the rule book, just text. Twelve solid pages of text. By the time I get to page three, confusion ensues around the table. Somehow the rules I am reading don't make any sense.

Someone suggests just making up our own rules so we can start playing. Others vote this suggestion down. Arguments take over, killing the initial enthusiasm about this game. Looking around the table I start to understand why World War Two broke out in the first place. After an hour of struggling with the twelve-page rule book, we scrap the game. The world war is postponed.

Lessons learned. Sometimes overcomplicating an experience is not the best idea. Some games do a great job introducing you gradually to the game flow via four phases: discovery (wow, this looks cool!), onboarding (okay, what I am doing here?), scaffolding (what's the best strategy to win?), and endgame (how to beat everyone?).

In each phase, your needs are different. Settlers of Catan is a great example. When you play it for the first time, you may just set the board as it comes by default, and play one game. As you get the hang of it, you can now build a strategy (go for longest route or invent?). If you're good at it, there are extensions to make the gameplay more challenging (ships, market, etc.). We've found that Settlers of Catan is one of the best board games to play with friends. Red wine adds another layer of fun. When designing learning, you may want to use the same concept, sans the wine. Instead of explaining everything on slide 1, introduce participants to features gradually. Start by grabbing their attention (discover) with something they can relate to in the form of a challenge. Give them an early success! Then, continue with onboarding (the idea being, now that you're hooked, here's some more). Unlockable items raise curiosity. Chunk the experience into smaller quests within longer challenges and celebrate success. The key is to challenge them, not frustrate them, in the scaffolding phase. And that's why gameful design is hard. That's why you have a lot of theory out there and less practice and examples. There's no way to learn gameful design other than by doing it. It's like riding a bicycle.

And by the way, back to my story with Axis and Allies. After everyone abandons my table, I start putting back everything to the box and I see something at the bottom …

It's a giant rule book. Now I'm confused. Rules? What were we reading then for twelve pages before? I look at the twelve-page document again, and I realize the title is "Clarifications to the Rules."

Keep it simple, folks! Just keep it simple! One rookie mistake instructional designers make is overcomplicating the gameful aspect of learning, trying to make it fun. If there is a gameplay, it must be as simple as it can be!! Period. But not simpler, as Einstein said.

Sharon Boller and Karl Kapp have a great book on designing learning games, if you're interested in a deeper dive: *Play to Learn*. You might also want to check out An Coppens's framework.[14]

MENTAL TRAVEL: Kevin Werbach's G.A.M.E. Workshop, 2015
(Where I Don't Want Learning to Stick.)

It is in November 2015 that I find myself in the room with the brightest in the game and gamification worlds. Researchers and practitioners gather to discuss "Gameful Approaches to Motivation and Engagement" at the Wharton School of Business, University of Pennsylvania. Kevin Werbach, whose gamification course on Coursera has been taken by hundreds of thousands of people, opens the workshop. Next to me sits Sebastian Deterding. If you've ever googled the definition of gamification, you probably found his definition in your search. There's more to that.

---

14   Deterding, S., Khaled, R., Nacke, L. E., and Dixon, D. (2011, May). "Gamification: Toward a Definition" in Proceedings of CHI 2011 Gamification Workshop (pp. 1-4). Vancouver, BC, Canada; https://gamificationnation.com/learning-gamification-framework/ to learn about motivation.

His paper "Gamification: Toward a Definition" gives you good foundations of the terminology and concept.[15]

But this story isn't about my table; it's about a product you can't buy. In good, cross-table fashion, I have a great conversation with Amy Jo Kim (game designer, author, and CEO of Shufflebrain) about her approach of effectively building products via application of game thinking. She's an inspiration to me and how I look at learning, from a product perspective via game thinking. At least, that's what I am thinking as I'm going through her inspiring examples.[16] Kim's game thinking approach helps to effectively build products customers want. So, I think to myself, *what if learning is a product? A product you can't buy. Only gain.*

But then I realize I am wrong.

Learning is the **process** to get to the product you can't buy. And the product is actually **knowledge**. However, a product sitting on a shelf that nobody is using is, well, useless. Literally. So, learning is a process that results in a product, which is knowledge. A product that you can't buy, you can only gain. (Better yet, the process of gaining knowledge doesn't have to be extremely painful, corporately controlled, and boringly long.)

However, gaining knowledge as a product isn't enough. The **application** of the product, in other words, the transfer from the shelf to practice, is a **skill**. Skills you master by practice. Sharpening your skills then prepares you for the ultimate challenge: **performance**. That is the demonstration of the skill, measured by key performance indicators (KPI). That is where your product meets your customers' needs. It's not about how many people launch a course. It's about how many of them close it and put it back to the shelf—unused, unpurchased, unappreciated!

Your ultimate goal is to create wearable products via learning. Because you don't want learning to stick. You want people to stick with learning.

Game Thinking focuses on the actions your customers need to take to be able to perform. Meanwhile, the traditional content-driven approach many times ends up short, with the product left sitting on a shelf. Yes, it may have a comfortable shelf life, but believe me, the Returns Department is a grim place of work. Don't work for the Returns Department! Build wearable products people will stick with!

---

15   http://www.academia.edu/33801825/Gamification_Toward_a_definition.

16   http://getting2alpha.com/breakthrough/.

MENTAL TRAVEL: Monica Cornetti's Radio Show, 2016 (Where we talk MVP.)

I had the pleasure of contributing to Monica Cornetti's "Gamification" radio show. Our topic title was "Game Thinking and the MVP of Instructional Design."[17]

Feel free to listen to the whole thirty minutes; but be forewarned we were all over the board. One of the things we discussed was what usually instructional designers ask who are interested in gamification:

"I read articles, books, and listen to TED talks. But how do I start gamifying my content?"

What Lies Beneath?

Learner engagement is one of the most elusive challenges instructional designers face, and they face it daily.[18] On the surface, it seems an easy problem to tackle: let's make learning fun! The problem, however, lies beneath the surface. Literally, in how our brain receives, registers, and processes information; how we are motivated. Research shows that games can be effective in raising learner engagement, but only if applied properly. Karl Kapp's "Once Again, Games Can and Do Teach!" provides a framework of a systematic approach of game thinking for instructional designers to go beyond the surface.[19]

The Angle of Implementation

To answer the question about where to start gamifying content, we need to step back for a second, and look at the bigger picture:

---

17   https://thegamificationreport.blogspot.com/2016/07/game-thinking-and-mvp-of-instructional.html

18   https://elearningindustry.com/5-design-steps-learner-engagement-humans.

19   https://www.learningsolutionsmag.com/articles/1113/once-again-games-can-and-do-teach.

Game Thinking for L&D ENGAGE THE WORL&D!

Self-Determination Theory
Art & Science
of motivation and engagement.

CONTENT Gamification
Modify learning assets or design new content to support motivation within the learning experience.

Game-based assessments
Learning games, templates, quizzes to assess knowledge or skill previously gained.

STRUCTURAL Gamification
No learning content change. External motivation to complete training.

Serious Games
Learning games to teach new knowlege or skills via interactivity and feedback loops.

NO Gameplay
Game mechanics to support motivation to change behavior.
Extrinsic vs. Intrinsic Motivation

Action-Driven Design
User to make meaningful choices, followed by consequences and positive feedback loop. Instructional Design focus shifts from content to action.

Gameplay
Game mechanics to support learning via interaction.
Mechanics-Dynamics-Aesthetics Framework

Evolution Need Over Time: Exploring => Onboarding => Scaffolding => Mastery

The WORL&D, a systematic approach to game thinking for L&D, is to provide guidance on implementation of game thinking in practice. The framework considers game thinking for L&D to be the overall action-driven instructional design approach, while gamification and game-based learning represent the implementation of that thought process.

The framework asks not whether instructional designers should design and implement either gamification or game-based learning (discrete), but, rather, how to define the angle (continuum) that supports the performance goals most efficiently. You may end up with gamification, you may end up with serious games, or, you may end up with neither. It's all about the right angle.

Four Main Areas of the WORL&D

The angle of implementation within the WORL&D framework can vary between 180 and 0 degrees. The closer the angle to 180 degrees (left), the more your implementation looks like pure gamification without gameplay. The closer the angle is to 0 degrees (right), the more your implementation looks and feels like a serious game with gameplay. In any case, the purpose of the implementation is learning, NOT entertainment.

Gamification

Karl Kapp distinguishes between structural and content gamification.[20] In structural gamification, you don't change or redesign the content itself. Content gamification, on the other hand, has added game mechanics inside the course.

Think of structural gamification as external incentives (often referred to as extrinsic motivation). You get a badge if you pass a course; you get points for watching on-demand video clips, etc. The content inside the course or video has nothing to do with the external gamification effort.

Content gamification, on the other hand, is about altering or designing the course itself to make the user experience more engaging and motivating. This time, the course has additional game mechanics, such as levels or quests. You might stumble upon an Easter egg, some unexpected surprise that makes you want to explore more. Content gamification requires much more effort to do right, but it can also balance the extrinsic and intrinsic motivation. There's still no definite gameplay. The course itself feels like a game, but usually there's no win or lose end status.

Game-Based Learning

On the right side of the WORL&D, users experience gameplay. Nicole Lazzaro talks about gameplay as the key to understanding different types of fun users experience when playing a game.[21] Gameplay introduces new elements: a start and an end with a clear result of a win or lose state. Note that not all games are competitive. In fact, the best game implementations for learning are collaborative, since that is more likely a desired behavior at work. While gamification feels more like a process that is gameful; gameplay is an event with a distinct start and end.

---

20   Kapp, K. M., Blair, L., and Mesch, R. *The Gamification of Learning and Instruction Fieldbook: Theory into Practice* (New York: John Wiley & Sons, 2013); also see: http://karlkapp.com/two-types-of-gamification/.

21   http://www.nicolelazzaro.com/the4-keys-to-fun/

Gamified Assessments

Gamified assessments are games users play to reinforce previous knowledge or skills. It's also used for pre-assessments, to analyze the knowledge or skill gaps. While gamified assessments have a feedback loop, their main purpose is to assess or reinforce already gained knowledge or provide practice for skills, NOT teach something new. Think of *Jeopardy*-style games and quizzes.

Serious Games

Serious games are at the very end of the WORL&D on the gameplay side. The sophistication and complexity of these games may vary, from tabletop to immersive 3-D environments. Overall, the goal is to learn through the user experience while interacting with the content. The engagement factor doesn't come from the number of game mechanics applied to learning. In fact, including multitude of game mechanics may even backfire. Remember, the ultimate goal of the WORL&D framework is for users to learn not to be entertained. The fine balance of engagement and evidence-based learning is key to a successful implementation. Expect lots of iterations and playtests before the final product!

Tip: One major factor often overlooked when gamifying learning is maintenance. Unlike games, learning content changes all the time. Keep in mind that the maintenance cost, required resources, and flexibility of the gamified solution all contribute to success in the long run. One of the best approaches to complexity is to create a gamified framework, where content is somewhat separated and can be easily updated, but the two seamlessly work together for the user.

Overview of Underlying Principles in the WORL&D

This is a high-level overview of related areas of motivation, user types, and player's journey from the world of gamification.

Self-Determination Theory

Self-Determination Theory (SDT) is the theory of motivation.[22] Design your learning to reach a balance of motivating forces: Autonomy, Relatedness, and Competence (ARC). Gamification expert Andrzej Marczewski proposes the RAMP approach for intrinsic motivation: Relatedness, Autonomy, Mastery, Purpose.[23] In L&D, designers often use Keller's ARCS (Attention, Relevance, Confidence, and Satisfaction) model[24]. Yu-kai Chou's Octalysis framework comprises eight core drives that motivate users.[25] Daniel Pink's Drive is also essential to understand to get beyond the surface.[26]

While the perspectives might be different in the models above, they all approach motivation as a complex, human-centered question. Digging deep in the topic, you may find the engagement and motivation is both art and science.

Game Thinking: Art and Science

Game thinking is the art and science of motivation and engagement via applied game elements and design. As mentioned before, I had a chance to attend the G.A.M.E. (Gameful Approaches to Motivation and Engagement) summit with Kevin Werbach in 2015, where researchers pointed out that current meta-analysis on gamification studies is inconclusive, we need more time. At the same time, practitioners agreed that we can't wait sixty years for a proof. In other words, we might not design the perfect solution today, but if it's working better than what we have now, let's do it!

---

22   http://selfdeterminationtheory.org/theory/.

23   Marczewski, A. *Even Ninja Monkeys Like to Play: Gamification, Game Thinking and Motivational Design*. CreateSpace Independent Publishing Platform, 2015), pages 65-80.

24   https://elearningindustry.com/arcs-model-of-motivation

25   http://yukaichou.com/.

26   https://www.ted.com/talks/dan_pink_on_motivation?language=en.

Action-Driven Design (as Opposed to Content-Driven)

Pitching action-driven design might be challenging for instructional designers when working with SMEs and stakeholders. Gamified solutions require the user/player to make decisions, act, and receive meaningful constructive feedback (positive feedback loop). The engagement comes from interacting with the game as a system, NOT from the content itself. Games are engaging, but watching people play games may not be (although, there's twitch TV for that, so who am I to judge).

How do you boil down content to actions? Use Cathy Moore's action mapping process.[27]

Gameplay or No Gameplay?

Focus on the user experience: does actual gameplay support your performance goal? If not, do not complicate the learning risking cognitive overload. Decide if users will actually play a game! Design. Create a prototype and playtest. Tweak. You might end up with a gameful/playful activity that is quick, flexible, and just as effective as an entire game. Remember: If you start a project with the end goal to build a game, you *will* build a game. And you might not need it at all.

Start with Game Thinking in mind, not with a solution in mind! Apply action-driven instructional design and decide the angle that best supports the performance goals. You may end up with gamification, game-based learning, simulation, or just a gameful/playful activity.[28]

27   http://blog.cathy-moore.com/
action-mapping-a-visual-approach-to-training-design/.

28   Nicholson, S. "A User-Centered Theoretical Framework for Meaningful Gamification" presented at Games+Learning+Society 8.0, Madison, Wisconsin, June 2012.

Practical Suggestions:

Do not start gamifying your content!

Game Thinking is a systematic approach you apply to the design of a learning experience via ACTIONS. If you start with the content first, and then try to sprinkle some game mechanics on top, you will most likely just use points, badges, and leaderboards only.

INSTEAD: Start with your business/performance goals (not learning objectives). Each of them may require a different approach. The obstacalities that hold people back from achieving those goals determine the angle above. Some problems won't need any training at all. Some will require motivational nudging. Some skill practices.

Start with PEOPLE

Game Thinking puts the **USER EXPERIENCE** in focus, via meaningful choices that users must make through actions. And for that, you will need users first, not content. (Don't get me wrong, you still need solid content, but if you let the content fill out the "seating time," you end up with no actions at all.)

INSTEAD: Start with early adopters. Find people who are interested in gamification, game design, game mechanics. Not everyone should be in your inner circle, though! You must trust these people. Why? Because you will need them to be completely honest with their feedback when playtesting your prototype. Create your club. Meet regularly and playtest. You'll be amazed how much your design improves before you take it to the SMEs and stakeholders.
Working with tons of learning vendors over the last decade as a business stakeholder, one thing always struck me: speed. By the time I saw something built as a prototype, it was way to late to change anything. The answer was that we're now in development phase, and the design has been approved. Don't let your stakeholders build something in their mind, it may not match what you were thinking of.

INSTEAD: To be the MVP (most valuable player) of the game, you might need to start building MVPs (minimum viable product)! The purpose of an MVP is not to wow the world with perfect instructional design. The purpose is to replicate quickly the experience, so you can playtest it. Get feedback. Tweak. And repeat.

Finally: start playing games!

All kinds of games. Analyze them: What makes them tick? How do you win? What makes them engaging? How does the difficulty change over time, as you get more experienced? What decisions do you have to make? What actions do you take? What consequences do you face? What motivates players not to quit?

Even if you conclude that your goal will be achieved via gamification (without building an actual game), you still must be familiar with game mechanics, how they work together (dynamics) and what effect you can achieve with them (aesthetics).

Amyg D'la Flow

LI DOE sits silently at the edge of the creek. Across the creek a White Bunny is hopping.

White Bishop: "There you are! Testing the waters?"

The Bunny runs away. LI DOE gives the Bishop a nasty look.

LI DOE: "Are you always so loud?"

White Bishop: "Comes and goes. Are you looking at the creek?"

LI DOE: "Kind of. It reminds me of something."

White Bishop: "That's natural here. Long-term memory."

LI DOE: "Reminds me of little things. Reminds me of how little things can make a big difference."

White Bishop: "Like what little things?"

LI DOE: "Little things that you don't even notice until they're gone."

White Bishop: "Like a semicolon at the end of the JavaScript line?"

LI DOE: "Kind of. Speaking of little things, the other day, I heard a wolf howling but it appeared to be ..."

White Bishop: "Fox? Red Fox?"

LI DOE: "How do you know?"

White Bishop: "We need to Go!"

MENTAL TRAVEL: New Hire Program, 2010ish (Where little things can make a big difference.)

Human-Centered Design places the user experience at the center of problem-solving. You must know your audience. The more familiar you are with the everyday lives of your target audience, the more successfully you can design learning for them.

Imagine a call center new hire training where you literally read through what kind of payment customers can use to access their bill: credit, debit, lockbox, phone, etc. Painfully dry documents. Human-Centered Design shifts focus from the processes and systems to the user experience. As a customer, I have preferences for how and when I like to pay my bill. The agent should be able to offer the matching payment option. Now, it's not only about the different type of payment options (knowledge problem) but application of the knowledge by matching the customer's story with the most appropriate type (skill).

Your practice exercise should be as close to reality as possible. So, the obvious design for payment options would be a scenario-driven call center simulation. As a designer, your job is to identify the performance objectives, so you can build learning objectives. In this payment scenario, the skill agents need to practice is active listening skills (listen for cues), and matching skills (knowledge of payment types).

Repetitive skill practice is a good candidate for a gameful learning experience. The proposed eLearning course is a drive-through, where cars pull over at the window and beep. You listen to their scenario and, based on customer's needs, suggest the payment type. If your suggestion resonates, you collect money (*ka-ching* sound effect).

What if agents weren't familiar with the process yet? Well, the eLearning has two modes: training and assessment. In training mode, you get feedback on your choices. So, by selecting the wrong choice, you get specific feedback on how to adjust. You learn. Once you were comfortable with the challenge in training mode, you can go to the assessment mode. Assessment mode is the same gameplay, except you don't get constructive feedback on your incorrect choices until the very end.

Now, is a drive-through a realistic scenario for a call center agent? Some stakeholders were not sure if agents takes this seriously, since it has nothing to do with being on the phone in a call center.

And this is where a small, realistic thing can make a big difference. I can't stress it enough how important it is to know your target audience. To observe how they work, what they do. If you have ever observed a call center agent, you know the magic moment when the beep sounds in their headsets. A customer is on the line! The agent's posture, face, and whole demeanor suddenly changes. Building on that critical moment, we replaced a generic car beep with a sound that was very close to the beep agents hear when a customer is on the line. As we piloted the experience, the feedback was all great from the participants (in fact, other tenure agents wanted to try it as well). A little (but extremely important) beep made a huge difference. You can't build realistic VR experiences for everything you design. Knowing your audience, however, can guide you to little things that can make a big difference in the design.

Darkness in the WORL&D

Bishop and LI DOE are playing Go. Despite the seemingly simple rules, Go is a complex game, even more complex than chess.

White Bishop: "It's getting late. One more riddle for you: I am one in four. Who am I?"

LI DOE makes the winning move.

LI DOE: "One in four? Are you 25 percent?"

LI DOE had no idea why he said that. His algorithm made a joke. Maybe this is deep learning. Anyway, the Bishop thinks this is the funniest thing ever from a Pawn. Deep learning burst into the mainstream media when in 2016 Google's AI beat the best human player in the world in Go. The significance of this achievement may not be obvious for all. This wasn't a brutal-force preprogrammed strategy. AI acted like a human: learned, trained, and built out its own conservative strategy. It first studied thirty million positions from expert games, then it played against itself across fifty computers, improving with each iteration, a technique known as reinforcement learning. Deep learning is using neural networks with multitudes of layers and connections between neurons.

Is AI beating us humans? Yes, in many ways. But when you hear stats like one in four Americans is unaware that the Earth orbits the Sun, you might think AI doesn't need that smart of an algorithm.[29]

Did you know that one in four Americans is unaware that the Earth orbits the Sun?

That's 25 percent! So, which one sounds more frightening to you? One in four or 25 percent? Or quarter of the population?

Does It Make any Difference?

Mathematically, it's the same value. However, the perception of value for humans presented with stats could be dramatically different. If the survival rate is 80 percent, it sounds good. But that also means two in ten people die. You can't visualize 80 percent of people. But when someone says ten people, you actually think of real people in your life: family, friends, co-workers ...

While the examples above are mathematically the same, wording can also make an actual difference in you're not careful. Let's look at a mundane example: you must complete 85 percent or more to get credit for a course. Why not 80 percent? Maybe your stakeholder wants to show tough love. Now, if you have questions in the quiz, and they are worth the same amount of points, what's 85 percent?

It's 8.5 questions. You can't pass 0.5 question. Which means you must pass 9 questions. So, technically, your passing rate is 90 percent.

If that's what you mean, use the simplest way of letting the learners know: You can only miss one question!

It's now getting dark in Hippo Campus.

White Bishop: "It's time for you to add Human-Centered Design to your collection."

LI DOE: "Is there a confirmation of learning?"

White Bishop: "It's dark. That means it's about to face the elimination challenge."

LI DOE: "You know I'm a Pawn with limited thinking, right?"

White Bishop: "Hmm ... It doesn't matter who you are, flatmate! What matters is what you can recall and apply. I want you to go back to

---

29   http://time.com/7809/1-in-4-americans-thinks-sun-orbits-earth/.

your long-term memory, and recall a dover sole moment."

LI DOE: "Dover sole? You mean cooking fish?"

MENTAL TRAVEL: Boston, 2014
(Pack you knife, and go!)

Top Chef has been one the few shows my wife and I have followed consistently. Some of it is about our appreciation for great food, good wine, and excellent conversation around the table. So, we thought it be a good bonding experience to introduce our teenage daughter to *Top Chef*. Last year we tried. Sophie, our daughter, watched the first episode and loved it. Until the very last scene.

Yes, the famous line when one of the contestants was sent home:

"Pack your knives and go!"

Sophie said that "the judges were very mean to the cook, who did try really hard, they just didn't appreciate it. They should have just warned him, and give him a second chance. This show is mean." She never watched it ever again.

Top Chef is a gamified cooking competition. Seemingly, it is about cooking fast, creatively, and efficiently under time pressure. But that's not what made my daughter like the show in the first place. It was the people in it. Like one of our favorite "characters"" from Season 11, Stephanie Cmar (who I met in person).

It's people and their struggle to succeed that keeps us glued to the show, the emotional connection we feel (even if the only creative culinary thing we've ever tried is a vague attempt at steaming cucumbers). Viewers almost feel like we're responsible for their career!

Why? Blame it on empathy! We compete every single day. We know how hard it is to perform under time pressure, in the spotlight, and with limited resources. Oh, and the mystery ingredients! Project changes, bad bosses, lame managers. And we know what it feels like to face the mean judges. We know what means to lose from time to time.

We Bounce Back

But we bounce back. A wise man once said: When you hit rock bottom, pick up something from the floor that might be useful later and spring back on! Cmar knows what it means to bounce back, as she was sent home way too early in the prior season because "her cauliflower soup did not have enough cauliflower in it." Here's how she describes the experience:

"It took me literally almost a year to really get over it. I've been traumatized by cauliflower ever since. It was one of my favorite vegetables, and now I am just getting back to eating it again."

She returned and did a phenomeal (made-up word merging "phenomenal" and "meal") job on Season 11. Our family also gave her the "personality of the season" badge. Good news! If you've ever been traumatized by cauliflower, there's hope. You can read more Cmar in her interview with "Eater."[30]

Gamified Cooking

As I said before, *Top Chef* is a gamified cooking competition. Let's look at five gamification "ingredients" that they use to make it exciting:

Core Loop

A core loop is at the heart of every gamified activity. It's the action you do over and over again. It must be simple to understand but complex enough not to become boring. In *Top Chef*, it's obviously cooking. What changes are the variables: time limit, resources, group or individual, mystery ingredient, location, number of people to cook for, etc. When you design a gamified activity, you MUST get the core loop right! Playtest and tweak until the mechanics involved work smoothly. If it's too easy, people lose interest. Too complex, they get frustrated. Make it SIMPLE! For learning, your goal is the performance objective, not the fun factor.

---

30   https://boston.eater.com/2013/9/30/6363009/
no-9-parks-stephanie-cmar-discusses-top-chef.

Challenges

Each episode starts with a quickfire challenge. A quickfire challenge is a fast-paced (I would say crazy-fast) challenge to make something) With a twist. How it matters in the overall competition is that you can get immunity from elimination for one round by winning the quickfire. That is a huge advantage, because ONE mistake can send you home. It also sets up some drama among the competitors: when you have immunity, you have nothing to lose. Would you pull 100 percent in a group activity with your peers who are also your competitors if you have nothing to lose?

Strategy

In each episode, contestants need to decide how "creative" they get. How much risk will they take, based on what others are doing. You might play it safe and float around in the middle of the pack. Or you might be bold and try something new. Your approach is up to you, as a player. (And of course, with super-careful editing, the audience gets the inside scoop of their thinking. And surprise!, surprise is another gamification mechanic.)

Collaboration

While most of the time *Top Chef* is an individual competition, there are episodes when you work in a team and you must collaborate. You might think it's not as exciting as a cut-throat competition, but instructional designers can learn a lot from collaboration. First, collaboration is most likely what people need to do at work. And yet, we don't include enough collaboration in learning solutions; we focus more on competition. Second, you will see roles emerge right away when you put people in a team. Google had a fascinating article on trying to find the perfect way to form teams.[31] Some people take charge right away, some love to organize, some offer support. No matter what, they must believe in their plan and execute it flawlessly. Strategy is crucial here: the balance of creativity and execution. And don't forget:

---

31   https://www.nytimes.com/2016/02/28/magazine/what-google-learned-from-its-quest-to-build-the-perfect-team.html?_r=0.

overall, these people compete against each other. And if you have immunity, you won't go home no matter how you perform. See where it's going?

People

Among these, and other exciting gamification elements, there's one that sticks out and glues viewers to the TV: people. The contestants. Their stories, relationships, arguments, actions, and emotions. You see them taking risks, making meaningful decisions that lead to consequences (good or bad), all the while continuously getting feedback (good and bad). And you wish it was like that at your workplace.

Gamification of Learning Conclusion

When you design a gamified learning solution, don't start with gamification elements. Start with people: keep the focus on the player's experience. That's the glue! Think what risks they take in real life, and let them take it in the learning solution. Show the consequences they see in real life, and provide constant feedback. Don't make it too easy! Let them fail, but give them enough scaffolding to grow! Yes, it might lead to a more emotional experience than reading bullet points and standards of procedures. So what? There's recovery after cauliflowerification.

The lack of emotion in training is like throwing random, otherwise great, ingredients into a bowl hoping to win a quickfire challenge. And that is very unlikely. Like it or not, you do not have immunity. Cauliflowers are traumatizing everywhere! This is going to stop here and now. With you! Go, pack your knives, and show them what's cooking!

Dover Soles of the WORL&D

The White Bishop hops around and around again, shaking his head.
White Bishop: "That is not a Dover Sole Moment. And it's getting really dark. Think of something quick before the Red Foxes come out."
LI DOE: "Maybe those Red Foxes can catch some Dover sole?"
White Bishop: "Dover Sole Moment is a figure of speech here. It's

an event when someone tries to do something for the very first time. Do you remember any of yours?"

MENTAL TRAVEL: Massachusetts, 2001 (Dover Sole Moment. For real.)

In 2001, my wife and I live in Cambridge. We love good food, great wine, and good conversations. Sounds like I've said this already. Anyway, I have been in the States less than a year, and since my home country (Hungary) is landlocked, I decide I love seafood. Therefore, I start eating anything and everything that comes from the Sea (in retrospect, some things should remain under water). One night, we go to this French restaurant (Hammersley's Bistro) in Boston, and I order Dover sole.

While we are waiting, my wife points out a person at the table next to us. She says that person could be the President of the United States one day. That person is John Kerry. And guess what? He orders Dover sole as well! I instantly know my future in this country will be bright. This Dover sole thing just can't be a coincidence.

But my story isn't about John Kerry; it's about another human: the waiter. As my Dover sole arrives, it comes with two waiters. A younger, visibly shaken waiter and an expert standing right behind him. Now, serving Dover sole in classic French style is an art. Words cannot describe the precision moves you need to perform under strict time constraints and eyes of scrutiny.

The Art of Serving Dover Sole

The expert waiter explains that this fish is going to be the very first one for the young waiter. They ask for our permission to proceed. I believe everyone should get a chance, so I give the green light. The young waiter starts the operation. His hands are a little shaky, as he's focusing hard on every move. He will not make eye contact with us. The older water gives him encouraging looks and instant feedback. At the end of the operation the young waiter has a moment of relief, and they retreat to the kitchen. I guarantee he has a shot of tequila right there.

John Kerry (who, by the way, did not become President but, rather. Secretary of State) does not have the same experience. His waiter does the whole procedure with his eyes closed, standing on one foot, singing an Irish folk song. Okay, not really, but he could have if he had wanted to; he is a pro.

Dover Sole Moment

This happened more than a decade ago. The reason I suddenly remember is because the other day on a business trip to Atlanta, I am checking into a hotel when ...

The receptionist, Valeria, greets me politely and warmly. Then she looks down and frantically types. A gentleman standing behind her is softly whispering and pointing. It is clear Valeria is having a Dover Sole Moment. I am one of her very first customers. We go through the process step by step. Slowly and gradually. It takes maybe twice as long as usual. Time to time, the gentleman behind her intervenes. Valeria does a good job of not freaking out while typing and talking at the same time.

At the end, they thank me for my patience. I tell Valeria she did a great job. And I said, you know what, in two weeks, you'll be able to do this with your eyes closed. They laugh. Tequila shots all around. Not really.

And that brings me to the a-ha moment. We often forget about our Dover Sole Moments—the very first time you try something that requires a skill. The feeling that "you know what to do" but your brain is freaking out processing all the stimuli bombarding you from the environment. We often take things granted. We do things with our eyes closed. Remember the first time you tied your shoe? Biked? Drove? Next time you design learning, try to recall some of your Dover Sole Moments. Remember how hard it was to focus, how important it was to get instant positive feedback, to get encouragement from someone you trust?

Not every Dover Sole Moment ends well! But remember! Even if anything goes wrong during your Dover Sole Moment, you are still in a better place than the fish on John Kerry's plate.

Sunrise in the WORL&D

White Bishop: "LI DOE, you have earned the Human-Centered Design trait."

LI DOE: "That's it? That was the night?"

White Bishop: "Tonight is a micronight. But the Red King now knows you're after the spell. If you have what it takes to beat the Red King, you must flex your resilience muscles now, before it's too late."

IRL CHALLENGES:

1. Explore Design Thinking by taking and facilitating the Stanford University crash course.[32]

2. Share you experience with others (either online of offline)

3. Resist "gamifying content" next time someone wants a course to be engaging. Find meaningful ACTIONS that participants need to do in real life first, then match it with game mechanics that support that activity.

4. Play a new game every week. It doesn't matter what type of game. Answer three questions:

- Who am I in the game?

- What's my goal in the game?

- What makes the game engaging (or not)?

---

[32] https://dschool.stanford.edu/
resources-collections/a-virtual-crash-course-in-design-thinking

Chapter Five

ADAPTIVE RESILIENCE
(FROM PASSIVE RESISTANCE TO ADAPTIVE
RESILIENCE)

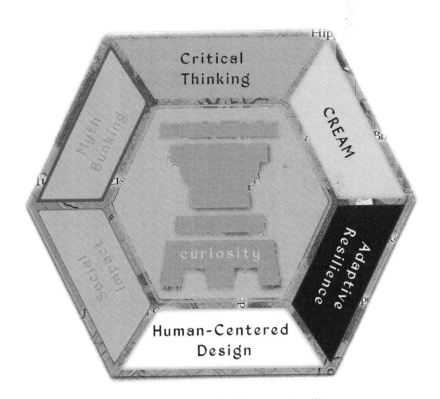

Pursuit of Trait 4/6: Adaptive Resilience

Where Are We?

Adaptive Resilience is the willpower source of the island. Most equipment and humans on the island run on willpower. This organic creature is a muscle itself. The more you use it, the stronger it gets. Over centuries, it has often changed the way it harnesses power. After major revolutions, it collapsed, but thanks to its adaptive resilience, it always bounced back, producing more willpower than ever. Humans come daily here to receive their willpower dose. There's a misconception about the resilience of this creature.

Adaptive Resilience isn't robustness that never tips over. Nor is it like the ability of a computer to restore itself after data corruption. The strength of Adaptive Resilience is its ability to adjust to change, to adapt and bounce back. Without adapting, it wouldn't be here today. By the way, did you notice the typo on the map? If not, your mind is playing tricks on you. Be careful, the Red King might already be in your head!

You may look at resilience as the strength to withstand all dangers by building a robust system with in-depth knowledge of a topic or skill. You might think if your expertise in the field has deep roots it will protect you from changes to come. In other words, you might think being good at any one thing is your insurance.

Robust-Yet-Fragile (RYF) is a term coined to describe systems that are robust against known dangers, yet vulnerable to the unknowns. For example, let's look at the internet. The very purpose of the internet was to ensure seamless communication in case of disaster. Information is traveling in packets. If one router is down or experiencing high traffic, the package is rerouted. It happens fast. You would never know that your emails have been all over the world.

And that robust structure works well against the danger of damaged servers. However, the very same feature allows hackers and spammers to bring down the system, not by damaging a server, but by flooding the system with empty pockets of information simultaneously, which is called the DDoS attack.

In real life, the art of bouncing back relies on your ability to strike balance between being robust and flexible. In the last decade, if you knew Adobe Flash very well, you were the King (or Queen) of eLearning development. How many Flash programmers are wanted today? Not many. When you build your portfolio, make sure you expose yourself to a variety of tools, methodologies, and processes. You don't need be a master of all, but you must be able to adapt as things change. Adapting takes time and effort; it's not like flipping a switch.

LI DOE's been moving around for a while on the map and can't find Adaptive Resilience anywhere. Can you help him locate the place on the map?

Our brain plays tricks on us all the time. Did you notice the typo in the name of the place? "Resilence" is missing a letter i. However, most people would never notice it, as our brain automatically corrects it. Optical illusions (such as the Roger Shepard's turning table in *Mind Sights: Original Visual Illusions, Ambiguities, and Other Anomalies*) work because our brain "corrects" what we see. We see the world as it is "supposed to be" based on our beliefs. Be careful with the Red King! Just because you see it doesn't mean it's true.

How Do You Build Resilience?

One of the biggest challenges about resilience is predicting the future of unknowns. Venturing into the world of unknowns is uncomfortable; it takes you out of your comfort zone. Stepping out of your comfort zone is like upping the weights in the workout. It hurts.

Stepping out of your comfort zone is like venturing into the dark. It has this distinguishable feeling of fear. Fear of failure. How often do you step out of your comfort zone?

MENTAL TRAVEL: Philadelphia, 2003
(Where I learn about the wine method.)

If you're a parent, you may know what it means to move your child to her own crib to sleep. There are hundreds of books on this subject: the four-, five-, and seven-step crib-training approaches. One is more painful than the other. I read them all. To my daughter to see if she likes any of them. Not really. Then we get a tip from one of our friends: the wine method.

Here are the steps of the wine method:

1. You grab a big glass of the wine of your choice.
2. You take that glass to the room where you put your child in the crib.
3. You establish a good night routine and firmly say good night.
4. You stay in the room with the child. And drink. Why? Because that child will scream and shake the gates of hell out of the crib. It will last about twenty to thirty minutes. (I bring a whole bottle of wine for the first time.)
5. Once the child is asleep, you can leave.
6. Next day, you repeat the same procedure. Including the wine. However, the fight gets shorter and shorter.
7. In a week, the child will simply go to sleep in the crib.

In a couple of days, it happened. I am sitting there with my big glass of wine and my daughter just goes to sleep. Now what? I finish the wine, of course.

A month later she knows the routine much better than we do, and sleeps in the crib with no problem. Funny thing is, even a year later, I bring my wine with me just in case. :)

How's Your Comfort Zone?

Let's face it, at least one time in your life you felt the urge to write a blog, make a video and post it on YouTube, post an article, author a book, or just ask something smart in a meeting, whatever. Then you heard the Red King's voice in your head:

"Why would anyone be interested in this? What if everyone already knows this? What if they laugh at my question?"

Suddenly, you see a nightmare scenario unfold in your imagination: your high school teacher pointing out your grammar mistakes, your first ex laughing at you while you pretend to be cool, your coworker who always knows a better way to do things, your epic bad hair day, Kim Kardashian smirking at your outfit. The returning nightmare of standing naked in front of a silent crowd under the spotlight realizing you're supposed to sing the national anthem in a stadium, and of course you remember neither the words nor the tune. We all have nightmares of failure.

As you postpone your creative actions, you feel good. For the moment, you're proud you even thought about stepping out of your comfort zone. And you're right! Exposing yourself by stepping out of your comfort zone could lead to a complete disaster and humiliation. Or not? Thing is, you will never know. However, based on statistics, it's more likely that there's someone out there who would be more interested in your thoughts than in seeing you naked in front of a crowd singing the national anthem.

How to Start a Blog Mentally?

So, here's a five-step process for stepping out of your comfort zone to start (v)blogging:

1. Grab your favorite inspirational drink (anything works, from fresh-squeezed grass to margarita cocktail).

2. Write about something you're passionate about. Not what you think people want to know! Here's a simple way to decide: If someone reading/watching your post wanted to know more, would you be happy to chat about the topic? If yes, go for it.

3. Did I say to drink at #1? No. I said grab it!! Get ready. Here's #4:

4. Ask someone you trust to look at your very first (v)blog. Ask them to give the thumbs up (or down) for publishing. Why? A friend's feedback is always extremely biased. They will give you the thumbs up. (If not, tweak it anyway. Drink!) So, what's the point of sharing then? You have just shared your thoughts. You have an audience. You are a (v)blogger! Congrats! Drink! The difference now is just the number of followers.

Find your voice! Write every day. Even if for just five minutes. Use your voice and listen to the echo. Write. Repeat.

And if all of this still hasn't convinced there is an audience for every school of thought, consider this: one of the most-watched YouTubers in 2016, PewDiePie, makes like $15 million a year by recording himself playing video games. Another high-paid YouTuber, a mystery woman, unwraps Disney toys on her channel for about $4.9 million a year. They have millions of subscribers.

My daughter laughed at me when I said I created my own YouTube channel, and I already have seven subscribers (by now it has surged to forty-six). Resilience is not doing something perfectly! Resilience is building a portfolio of capabilities, so when things change (and they will), you can adapt, navigate, and not fall. It's about building out your hexagons to tessalate your career-board. The more options you have, the more likely you can move to the next phase in your career.

Passing Adaptive Resilence in the WORL&D, walking toward the Dunes of Obstacalities, there's a patch of desert. It's hot and dry like any other desert. This is where LI DOE runs into a naked man. Yes, you heard right. A naked man in the desert. He's using his hand and head only. He's an architect. LI DOE turns back before catching the dangerous Naked Architect in the Desert Syndrome (NADS).

MENTAL TRAVEL: College Years, 1990 (Are you suffering from NADS?)

NADS originates from my first college experience, where I studied to be an architect. For three whole weeks. Technically, one of the weeks is a freshman summer camp, so two weeks for real. Leaving that college behind is one of the best decisions in my life. And the reason I left is NADS.

There's this professor who teaches us the basics of architecture: how to design, by that I mean how to draw. So, day 1 he tells us to be prepared:

"An architect is an architect. You're going to use your head and your hand only. Nothing else. If you're naked in the desert, you will still know what to do, because I'm going to make sure it's all in your head and hand."

Now, I'm not sure what picture this scene conjures in your mind, but in my mind I see a naked architect in the desert using only his head and hand. In week 1, I started to wonder: how often do architects end up naked in the desert where they need to design a house without any tools or resources? But again, this is my first college experience. So, I figure that's how the cookie crumbles. The professor gives us homework at the end of week 1: draw squares. Fifteen different squares on a piece of paper. They all have to be perfect lines. But here comes the catch: we must use actual INK to draw the lines and then, PAINT the squares inside with watercolor!

If you've ever tried mixing straight lines, ink, and watercolor, you know what I'm talking about. If any of the lines gets blurred (any of the fifteen squares), you have to start the whole page again. I've hated Tetris ever since.

That's when I decide to leave this profession behind. But, I learn something from this experience. NADS is an interesting phenomenon. People who exhibit NADS believe that you must memorize everything in your head, like "in the old days." How often does it happen that you need to design or take a course that forces you to memorize things? Do you really need to recall all that information at work?

Don't get me wrong. In an emergency situation, I don't want people to ask Siri whether they should cut the blue or red wire while diffusing a bomb. But ask this question a lot: how often does this situation happen to you? To the target audience at work? What tools and resources do they need to deal with the situation? What's the actual risk of not remembering?

One of the problem with NADS is that by forcing you to memorize things, it gives false confidence that you can do it, without help, without tools, and nobody can take it away from you. Whatever "it" is. You become Mr. Robot. Executing the code flawlessly.

Until something changes! Because in reality, NADS takes away your agility to think and adapt. You lose one of the most important competitive advantages of today's WORL&D: adaptability. Without knowing how and why you make decisions, you shut out the environment and just follow steps. If anything changes in the environment, you still follow the same steps. Mechanical robots follow preprogrammed instructions no matter what. They're precise, quick, and never get tired. Perfect! Unless something changes in the environment. That can be lethal. Google the story about the robot from section 130 that entered section 140.[33] Same job, wrong place.

In contrast, at another college, that I *do* finish, one of my professors has all of his exams open-book. He gives out challenges weekly that make us think and apply knowledge. He teaches us problem-solving by giving tools and methodologies, rather than templates and step-by-step instructions.

After twenty-five years in this profession, I can tell you: the chances that you need to problem-solve and adapt your way of thinking are much higher than ending up naked in a desert designing a house with your bare hands. Watch out for the symptoms of NADS!

One practical check is to tell the why, not just the how. "Experts" often skip the why, because in their mind, decision-making is so entrenched that they are not even aware of making decisions anymore. Focusing on the why is the foundation of adaptability. Like the good foundation of a house designed by architects who may or may not have been naked in the desert. Ever.

Feedback, Please!

Have you ever been in a situation when someone "opened up the floor" for feedback, so they can improve? Except, when you give them feedback, they have an answer as to why it didn't go well. They get defensive. When you ask for feedback, take that feedback as a gift.

That's easier said than done. Getting feedback on a piece of work you are emotionally attached to is hard. I write my first screenplay in 2000. When submitting to a competition I'm convinced that I just bought my ticket to Hollywood. Then I receive the feedback (that I paid an extra $70 for). The judge's feedback starts something like this:

"Excellent start. You suck the reader in right away! The end? With the twist? Absolutely, sixth-sense... But man, what a pain to read in-between..."

I stop writing for a year after this review. After seventeen years, I still have that letter. Time to time, I read the words of the judge. He's right.

---

33   https://qz.com/931304/a-robot-is-blamed-in-death-of-a-maintenance-technician-at-ventra-ionia-main-in-michigan/.

Throwing ingredients into a bowl doesn't make you a cook, let alone a "top chef." Same goes for gamification: throwing exciting game mechanics and elements on top of each other won't cut it. Like adding all colors and transitions on one PowerPoint page. I made a mistake, I worked in a silo, all alone with no sharing or collaboration. My screenplay was something that looked like a movie I've seen on TV before.

The next five years I spend on Zoetrope.com, a peer-review site for all kinds of artists. Whether you write short scripts, songs, poems, whatever. You upload your art and get feedback from others who are in the same boat. Honest, brutal, straightforward feedback. In return, you do the same for them.

Sometimes, people completely misunderstand your writing. But that's okay. You know what? There are going to be people who will completely not get your creative eLearning course either. The only way to master the art of receiving and digesting feedback is to expose yourself (a positive spin on naked architect?). In a good way. Today, we call this work out loud.

After years of tweaking my writing, my next screenplay is a finalist in an international writing competition. So today, I want to thank anyone I've ever come across who has given me feedback on anything! Thank you, and please! Keep the gifts coming!

How to Be AAA-Rated?

Don't ever assume people don't need feedback! Often, we only comment when we are emotionally charged. A simple but meaningful comment like "Your post helped me do X ..." is a tremendous gift.

Recovering from negative feedback requires a good amount of resiliency. You must be able to look at the feedback from an objective standpoint. Accept, analyze, and adapt. There you go: AAA ratings. Accept the feedback. Analyze what you could do differently, what knowledge, skills, and motivation you need to improve. Unlearn some of the skills you have. Finally, adapt how you approach the next challenge.

After turning back from the desert, LI DOE finds herself in the middle of a dilemma: with four out of six traits under her belt, should she just face the Red King? He's got resilience; he can bounce back and adapt. LI DOE feels the urge to get promoted to Queen!

IRL CHALLENGES:

1. Start a blog (if you haven't already):

Select a topic you're passionate about!

Write a short blog

Find a person whose opinion you trust, and they can be honest with you: ask for feedback

Rewrite first draft

Publish your blog (Wordpress is one of the easiest way but there are numerous platforms out there)

Stick to a schedule to post (maybe once a month, or a week?)

2. Pick one of the suggestions from the article (Five Science-Backed Strategies to Build Resilience) to build your resilience![34]

Change the Narrative

Face Your Fears

Practice Self-Compassion

Meditate

Cultivate Forgiveness

---

34   https://greatergood.berkeley.edu/article/item/ five_science_backed_strategies_to_build_resilience

Chapter Five and a Half

COLLABORATION
(FROM PILLARS OF SALT TO PILLARS OF SAND)

With four traits under her belt, LI DOE decides to face the ultimate enemy: the Red King. It's time to visit the downtown the Training Czar Heights, the dreaded red Castle.

The Castle that sits on Training Czar Heights is the home of the Red King. Before the self-proclaimed takeover, the downtown area where the Castle stands used to be a blooming small business district filled with shops, cafes, and remote workers. The roots of the Castle are deeply entrenched in the spell. Rumor is, people often smell fresh-brewed coffee around the Castle, the reminiscent of an old diner. Pawns are not allowed inside. LI DOE's going to need all the knowledge and skills just to get close to the Castle. Many who tried to get promoted to Queen failed, and were taken off the board, so to speak. The land surrounding the Castle is nothing but a red chili pepper farm. The wild woods around the Castle is known for many Red Fox attacks.

After the eCurse, the self-proclaimed Red King ruled the WORL&D with an iron fist. He held the key to all knowledge and skills by launching an automated "wisdom watch group," called Learning Machine Scythe. The Scythe was used to harvest data on residents, to count how many times residents accessed learning content, who passed and who did not. "Out of Compliance" led to tragic events in the woods, and the Red King earned the nickname "Training Czar." The Scythe enforced the spell on the WORL&D. Time has slowed down so much, they're still in the medieval era, where no phones are allowed in the classroom. Rumor has it the SILO is filled with ILT classes, frozen in time, still under the dreadful spell of the Scythe.

The doom and gloom were palpable in the land, until one day, some brave pieces from the White family started a resistance. The constant mental battle for change has weakened the Red King, who is still clinging to his losing power. Today, more than ever, the Red King feels isolated between the cold walls under the lone red sky. Yes, indeed, the Red King used to own the WORL&D; he used to roll the dice. But now he's mostly wondering: What comes next? Robots? AI? Blockchain? Recent research by Coldplay discovered that, despite all the big impressions the Red King is making, his Castle actually stands upon pillars of salt and pillars of sand.

Upon aforementioned discovery, the Red King issued a rebranding order, stating that from now on the Castle is no longer a Castle, thereby solving the problem of the "Castle standing upon pillars of salt and pillars of sand." From now on it is a Rook, not a Castle. A handful of L&D folks, who resisted and wanted to speed up time are losing their battle with the Scythe. Those heroes are still in hiding. Who knows how long they can hold up in the SILO.

Don't be fooled. The Red King still has the magic red power; the evil source of the Scythe has just published its annual compliance report: "100 Percent Compliance." There are two ways to achieve that. Either convince everyone to be compliant or get rid of those who are not. I'll leave it at that.

And while LI DOE thinks she can convince the Red King she is worth promoting to Queen, the Scythe might think otherwise.

In the pouring rain, LI DOE stands in front of the giant Castle, holding his shield above his head as an umbrella. Somehow, the rain still gets through, but that's not what LI DOE is most concerned about. The Red King is nowhere in sight. In the woods nearby, we hear the ominous howls getting closer and closer.

LI DOE: "My name is LI DOE. I've collected four of the missing traits!"

A Red Fox appears at the edge of the woods. The beast's eyes are riveted at LI DOE. Lightning strikes right next to LI DOE. That scares the Fox away.

LI DOE: "My shield is already strong. I want to be promoted to Queen!"

On top of the Castle, the Red King appears, wearing the dark sunglasses in the rain. The Red King gestures, and the rain stops at once. At least above the Castle.

Red King: "There's already a Queen, my friend."

LI DOE lowers his shield to look at the Red King sipping his coffee. He dips something into the coffee, something that looks like chili peppers.

LI DOE: "It doesn't matter. You can have multiple Queens on the board."

Red King: "Wow, an ant with an attitude. I warned you once, LI DOE!"

LI DOE: "I want to get promoted to Queen! I want to go home. Back to my old world."

The Red King bursts out laughing.

Red King: "I still can't promote you to Queen."

LI DOE: "Why? I've escaped the SILO, destroyed Borg the shark, collected four missing pieces of the Magic Mojo Hexad!

Red King: "Oh, your magic mojo. Is that why you're not afraid of me?"

LI DOE: "My shield will protect me!"

Red King: "Protect you? Against the Scythe? Take one more step forward, and you'll see."

LI DOE steps forward with a grin.

LI DOE: "I want to be Queen."

The Red King gestures and the Scythe flies up in the air behind him. The Red King points at LI DOE. The Scythe attacks. LI DOE raises the shield to protect as the Scythe swings at her. As if the shield wasn't even there, the Scythe cuts through it and scratches LI DOE's face. Looking at what's left from the shield, LI DOE changes his mind and steps back.

Red King: "Your shield. Strong enough, eh?"

From the woods, tens of howling Red Foxes charge at LI DOE. The Scythe prepares to swing again. The Red Foxes surround LI DOE.

LI DOE: "Let's collaborate here!"

A lighting strike hits the ground with the biggest bang.

IRL CHALLENGES:

1. Sharing and Collaboration don't start with technology, it starts with a mindset. Start every meeting with at least one person sharing what they learned that day (or week)

2. Find out who's in charge of "Collaboration Technology" at the company. Have lunch or coffee with the person. Learn about their challenges.

Chapter Six

SOCIAL IMPACT
(FROM SILO TO WORKING OUT LOUD)

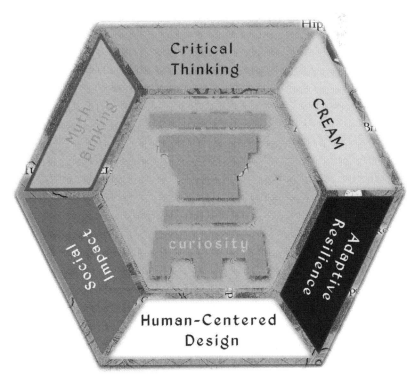

Pursuit of Trait 5/6: Social Impact

Where are we?

Rabbit O'Reg is a peaceful place. It's the home of Rabbit O'Reg, the oldest resident in the WORL&D. LI DOE opens his eyes and checks his body.

LI DOE: "Hey, did you do this?"

Rabbit O'Reg: "Did what?"

LI DOE: "Teleport me right before I was about to smack the Red King on the head?"

Rabbit O'Reg: "You can't smack him alone."

LI DOE: "I know, that's what I was focusing on! Collaboration features, not an old horse. No offense."

Rabbit O'Reg: "I know, I can read your mind."

LI DOE: "You can read my mind? What am I thinking now?"

Rabbit O'Reg: "The good old days."

LI DOE: "Wow. You're an honest man. You do read my mind."

Rabbit O'Reg: "You're safe here. That's the only place the Red King would not think to look. An old horse's house."

LI DOE: "Do you have a platform for me? With collaboration features?"

Rabbit O'Reg: "Platform with collaboration features?"

LI DOE: "Sure! I was focusing on an online platform with strong collaboration features. For my shield."

Rabbit O'Reg: "Collaboration features don't collaborate. People do. Speaking of your shield, this is the best I could do."

Rabbit O'Reg hands over the fixed shield.

LI DOE: "Wow! Like brand new. How did you do that?"

Rabbit O'Reg: "I've been here since before even Hill and Sea O'Rious landed. I was here before this place existed."

LI DOE: "How could you be somewhere before the place exists?"

Rabbit O'Reg: "Would you like a cup of coffee, perhaps?"

"Collaboration features do not collaborate. People do." — *Rabbit O'Reg*

MENTAL TRAVEL: Imaginary Meeting, 2000s
(Where we learn that as a group, we are always smarter and stronger than any one person in the room.)

You're in a conference room, ready to start your presentation on the quarterly TPS reports. It's a dry run before the real thing, the senior leadership meeting. Present: Busy Boss, Geek Peer, Marketing Mary, and Communication Craig. You're sharing your PPT on the webinar. And from there, it's going downhill.

```
INT. CONFERENCE ROOM -- DAY

Typical white conference room with just
enough chairs and barely enough cable to
connect to the projector. People stare at
the projector. Around table sit MARKETING
MARY, stylish, freshly 30. BUSY BOSS,
easing into the 50's, still dressing like
30. COMMUNICATION CRAIG, multi-device
intern-looking dude. GEEK PEER, corner
sitter, mindfully coloring.

                LI DOE
        (smiles as PPT shows up)
        Success!
```

                    MARKETING MARY
                       (snarky)
          That's not the latest
          template.

              All: jaws drop.

                      LI DOE
                 (losing confidence)
          Not? I used the one
          on the shared drive.
          It says latest in the
          file name.

Busy Boss fires up her laptop.

                    BUSY BOSS
          I have latest_
          version_3a.ppt. Let me
          send it quick.

             SOMEONE ON THE PHONE
          Ly.

                     LI DOE
          Hi, it's Li! Who's
          just joined?

             SOMEONE ON THE PHONE
          No, I mean quick-ly.
          Not quick. I was on
          mute.

All: nods.

COMMUNICATION CRAIG
Is that one legal
approved?

BUSY BOSS
How would I know that?

MARKETING MARY
Check slide 13. Is
the logo at the upper
left? Or the lower
right?

ALL
(in despair)
Lower right!

COMMUNICATION CRAIG
Hey! Fresh off the
press! I just the got
the latest from legal.
Sending it quick...
LY.

LI DOE
Great! I will just
import the style into
this one, so the
content is ready to
go.

                    SOMEONE ON THE PHONE
          Sorry, I was on mute.
          We need to rerun the
          analysis with the
          latest numbers on the
          pie chart.

                    BUSY BOSS
          Damn it.
               (silence ensues)
          I mean right. How do
          we do that?

                    GEEK PEER
          Frank used to do that.
          From the unified Excel
          sheet he created from
          the LMS query dump.

                    SOMEONE ON THE PHONE
          Frank who?

                    GEEK PEER
          Frank Tipton, the
          intern who left last
          week.

Beat.

                    COMMUNICATION CRAIG
          Let's find out if IT
          has wiped his laptop
          already!

                    LI DOE
          Done. Imported the new
          styles sheet.

               MARKETING MARY
          That logo above the
          chart is old. Need to
          replace it.

                  GEEK PEER
          That's an embedded
          screenshot with a pie
          chart. The whole page
          needs to be recreated
          with the new data.

            COMMUNICATION CRAIG
          Can we just cover the
          logo with a white
          rectangle?

                 BUSY BOSS
          White rectangle it is.

                 GEEK PEER
          But the data...

           SOMEONE ON THE PHONE
          Too late. They wiped
          the intern's laptop.

               MARKETING MARY
          What now?

```
        SOMEONE ON THE PHONE
        Photoshop. Need to
        drop now.

Beep.

        COMMUNICATION CRAIG
        Photoshop? Who the
        heck was that?
```

Is it On Your Hard Drive?

This is an excerpt from a white paper published a decade ago on "The High Cost of Not Finding Information:"

"IDC (International Data Corporation) estimates that an enterprise employing 1,000 knowledge workers wastes at least $2.5 to $3.5 million per year searching for nonexistent information, failing to find existing information, or recreating information that can't be found."[35]

Are We Doing Any Better Today? Your Call.

Why are we still not sharing information? Why are SILOs still out there? What happened to the promise of "computers" at the workplace to take over the mundane, mindless tasks, enabling people to focus on creative, innovative ideas? (Sounds like AI is promising that today.) How come computers and the constant network connections have not brought down those SILOs?

What Would Sharing and Collaboration Do at the Workplace?

"In organizations, [sharing and collaboration] make the walls between silos more permeable, helping talent pools connect and saving workers countless hours in looking for information." Jane Bozarth, Show Your Work

We learn by making mistakes. Sharing the end product is great, but you never know why decisions were made, what adjustments happened, why they ended up with a certain design. Without mistakes, there's no

35   http://www.ejitime.com/materials/IDC.

lesson learned. Once in a life, everyone, no exception, commits the mistake of hitting "Reply All." Yes, I know, it conjures endless giggles. We learn by making mistakes. Once you make that mistake, you double and triple check every email before you hit Send.

Narrating your work may sound surreal, almost like you're talking to yourself. On my blog, *Rabbitoreg,* I show various examples of how JavaScript can be used with the Articulate Storyline authoring tool. Most examples reveal the design behind the end results. Projects you work on never turn out the way they were designed in the beginning. Along the way, you make decisions and learn lessons. Most organizations consistently do post-mortem analysis about lessons learned. That's a good step toward recapturing learning takeaways. The question is, when I say the word "SharePoint," do you see a vibrant, social community sharing and revisiting those learning takeaways or a repository of files in folders that you can find only if you're a lucky person with the added support of a four-leaf clover in your wallet?

Don't get me wrong, I don't want to single out SharePoint or even the LMS. It's the incorrect implementation (or lack of implementation) that causes issues. My point is that collaboration and sharing are not about technology and collaboration features. When it's designed, controlled, and driven top-down by IT, it's unlikely that you end up a vibrant community. Oh, but you just rolled out the collaboration features? Too bad features don't collaborate. Features are not people. People collaborate. Until we're replaced by robots and AI, you'll need people to share and interact with each other. Humans are complicated. No wonder organizations have a whole department to deal with them (HR). Old habits die hard. Rolling out anything that changes our life will face resistance. An email to complete your profile and post at least one thing a day will not create collaboration, let alone a community. Create a safe place to build trust. Community grows on trust, not on tech. Show the value! Find the pioneers who want to share! Build the culture, and give them the intuitive tools to use. And if you do roll out a platform, please make sure all your senior leaders are using it. Otherwise, it's just another checkmark on someone's to-do list. Technology is never the answer. It's a vehicle to get to the destination, but you need a destination first. And with the vehicle and destination ready, you must make sure everyone is on board, before starting the ride.

MENTAL TRAVEL: Hungary, 1994
(Where I play a role in "The Lady of Larkspur Lotion.")

It is during my college years that I dabble in theater. In an English Language Drama Club, we're staging "The Lady of Larkspur Lotion" by Tennessee Williams. I play the role of a writer of some sort. It's a play about reality (cockroaches and rent) versus dreams. This writer character is supposedly working on a 780-page masterpiece, often waiting for the muse to show up at the bottom of liquor bottles. The play is about life, illusions, and the power of resilience.

Long story short, I have an emotional outburst in the play, which I conclude by drinking half of the flask I happen to find in my robe's pocket. We practice for weeks. Of course, I'm not drinking whiskey; we're using tea similar to the color of whiskey. Everything goes well, my emotional dialogue, drinking, drama.

Until performance day. About half an hour before start, someone knocks the bottle of "whiskey" down and it breaks into pieces. I'm already wearing my robe but we have no time to waste. I run to the nearest grocery store, looking for something that looks like whiskey. Now, this is in Hungary, where you can buy not only beer or wine but hard liquor in grocery stores. I buy a bottle of Hubertus.

Hubertus is 36 percent alcohol. I pour some out right before the play to be more realistic (no hard-core drinker carries a full bottle). And off we go ...

By the time I get to my emotional outburst on stage, I completely forget about this incident. After shouting and screaming at the landlord in the play, I pull the "tea" out and, as we practiced for weeks, I gulp half of it down. By the time I realize it's the 36 percent alcohol that's going down, it's too late. You can't get out of character on stage. No way.

After gulping down half the bottle I literally CANNOT SPEAK. Only hot air comes through my throat. It is a good ten seconds of silence before I can continue.

Funny thing is, after the play, some of the people in the audience said how effective that pause was. Little did they know it was exactly 36 percent effective.

How Does This Story Relate to L&D?

Life happens. There aren't templates for everything. No matter how much you practice and master your role, things change. Technology comes and goes. Often, learning theories are only sexy for L&D; the business does not care about them. You'll more likely be judged on your resilience and adaptability, based on how fast you react, and how effective you are at solving problems. The Red King throws all kinds of monkey wrenches at you. Whatever happens, DO NOT get out of character. Finish the play, then make a note. Lessons learned are gold! Don't forget to share your gold afterward!

Prepping for the ATD International Conference and EXPO in 2016, I decide to create some grass-roots gamification. I used a scavenger hunt / trivia mobile app to build an adventure called JAMES BOUND.

Participants had to find QR code locations, solve puzzles, even go to a location (Hard Rock Cafe) to get points and complete the hunt. The app used a GPS locator to track your position. Little did I know that Pokémon Go would steal my idea two months later. :)

But that's not the point here. Through that little gamification project, I met lots of people: gamification experts, game designers, L&D thought leaders. I also had the pleasure of talking to a lot of people at the conference who were new to instructional design. They all had the same question: how to break into this field. Most important, how to break the catch-22 of portfolio dilemma: I need a portfolio to get a job. I need a job to build my portfolio.

My Two Cents on Portfolios

Build Your PPT! Not a PowerPoint, but your People, Processes, and Tools.

People

Network. Follow people on social media to see what they see. Find a local chapter of learning geeks. Talk shop! Do not just rely on infographics floating around. Join a community like Articulate's E-Learning Heroes. It's not about the tool; it's about connecting with people, learning from people, and sharing good stuff. What if you don't know any thought leaders? For my trivia game, I reached out to people who have never met me and asked them to tell me a secret (I needed it for the trivia). You can't get more personal than that, and I received not one "how dare you?"

If you're looking for a strategic advantage, build your people skills as much as your process skills. Learn about negotiation, risk management, project management. While today you may see instructional designers working with "content" most of the time, in the future (IMHO), you'll have to be much more business focused. And that means dealing with difficult people. At the end of the book I have a suggested reading list if you're interested.

Processes

Learn more about ADDIE, Agile, SAM, and Cathy Moore's Action Mapping. Be familiar with gamification and microlearning, at least at a cocktail bar conversation level. You'll find that a lot of companies use some variation of these.

Tools

Download the trials for Articulate Storyline, Adobe Captivate, and Lectora. Again, you will probably run into one of these any place you go. But downloading the trial isn't enough. Build interactions. You don't need to build a whole course! Show in your portfolio that you can SOLVE BUSINESS PROBLEMS! Hiring managers care about your ability to work with others to quickly produce results. Business results. Not learning objectives.

In your portfolio, summarize the business problem, and then show how your solution addresses it! If you don't have any idea what business problems you should solve, go to LinkedIn, and ask people: give me a business problem you would love to solve at your organization. The point is don't just show the solution! Without knowing what the business problem was, your solution is just another drag and drop in the ocean.

Rabbit O'Reg brings a cup of coffee. LI DOE inhales the aroma.

Rabbit O'Reg: "Last cup of the fresh-brewed golden ever from the old diner."

LI DOE: "Last cup? What happened to the diner?"

Rabbit O'Reg: "It was destroyed."

LI DOE: "I don't drink coffee. But this one smells good. Really good."

In fact, LI DOE can't stop smelling it. He looks somewhat dizzy.

LI DOE: "I think it's bizarre that foxes howl here. What does a wolf do then?"

Rabbit O'Reg: "They're not foxes, they're Varks. Each has a different howling style: Visual, Auditory, Reader, and Kinesthetic. They're the Red King's boots on the ground. Viscous folks. Avoid them."

LI DOE: "Wow, bizarre. Okay, let's play one more time. What word am I thinking of?"

Rabbit O'Reg: "Bizarre."

LI DOE: "How are you doing that?"

Rabbit O'Reg: "Practice. Professional development. Strong coffee. Lots of afternoon naps."

MENT AL TRAVEL: Philadelphia, 2000ish
(In which we learn how bizarre professional development life can get.)

If the only time you brush your teeth is when you go to your annual dentist visit, you're going to have very few teeth and fewer friends very soon. Professional development is like dental hygiene. Own it. Do it. Daily. I'll say this only once!

I had a project management training once, because it is good to have project management knowledge, right? Right. Except, when you put people who think the critical path leads to the ER in the same room with people who have been using the Monte Carlo Simulation for risk assessment, you know what will happen.[36] Bizarre things will happen because nobody will be satisfied with the training.

How Bizarre?

The facilitator for that workshop is a particular individual exhibiting all symptoms of the classic ego-boosted blunt force trauma. He literally says:

"Now, I want you to grab your pens and write this down. This is very, very important. I'll say it only once. Again, it's very important. And guess what? It's not in the book!"

And I'm like: "Excuse me! So, we either hired the gatekeeper of all PM secrets here or whoever made this book forgot to include the most important thing! How bizarre."

The facilitator also insists that I should underline certain words. If I don't underline them, he says, I won't remember them. WOW! Could that be the bizarrest secret of all? <u>I've been typing everything underlined ever since.</u>

But in all seriousness, is it the problem of the PD content? Delivery? Vendor? Those of us who "read ahead in the book"? Should we just not learn anything until it comes to us packaged in a PD training course?

PD can be a huge motivator in the workplace (and I'm not even evoking the M word for a generation), but only if it's a good match with what humans actually want and need. I repeat: from the human's perspective, not from leadership's checkbox perspective.

So, unless you work with elephants, acrobats, lions, and monkeys, I would still suggest going full steam ahead!

Speaking of steam and monkeys. If you lived in nineties there's no way you avoided the hit song "How Bizarre" by OMC. My never-ending curiosity of what the heck this song was about drove me all the way to New Zealand. You might remember the music video: a '69 Chevy cruising with the singers, Pauly Fuemana and Sina Saipaia, in the back of the car; Brother Pele, the local DJ.

---

36   http://www.palisade.com/risk/monte_carlo_simulation.asp.

Except, it turns out, Brother Pele couldn't make it to the shooting, so that day some completely random person ended up in the car: a Filipino named Hill. He was knocking on the studio door that morning to see if he could assist in any way. Well, he did. They put him in the car and started shooting the video.

There you go. This is a song by Pauly Fuemanna, a former "gang member" who didn't master any instruments, could barely sing (you can see how the refrain is driven by the chorus), and wasn't the most dedicated worker. His talent was resilience. Simon Grigg, who was behind the song, has a great book titled *How Bizarre: Pauly Fuemanna and the Song that Stormed the World*. I know. On the surface, a one-hit wonder has nothing to do with learning, but I suggest reading the roller coaster story behind Pauly Fuemanna and "How Bizarre." This song was a brainchild of bizarre collaboration, drama, and dedication. Collaboration, drama, and dedication. Who says these three things are not exactly what L&D life is about? And remember, as a group, we are always smarter and more creative than any ONE person in the room.

Blue Sky Scenario

LI DOE opens his eyes. He's lying under the blue sky. He springs up. There's nothing like Rabbit O'Reg anywhere. The scenery is idyllic. A beautiful blue lake in the depth of a valley. LI DOE grabs his shield on the Social Impact trait. A letter is attached:

Dear LI DOE,

Let's talk about your personal brand! I still remember the first time I used a thermal camera. It was a hands-on session at college. We put our hands on the surface of a bucket of cold water. Then, after ten seconds, we lifted it up. And there it was: our palm print was still clearly visible for a long time through the thermal camera. Now, of course, with your naked eye, there was nothing to see but water.

I often think of personal brand in the same way. It's the energy footprint you leave behind when you're not even there anymore. Both digital and in real life (IRL). It's invisible, unless you have the sensitive equipment to view it. We humans all have that sensitive equipment. Every person in the room you meet virtually or IRL forms an opinion of you. The bad news is your personal brand is subjective, as if we all had our thermal camera calibrated differently. The good news is you can shape that energy footprint you leave behind.

Think of a brand you like! Car makers, electronics, fashion, food, whatever... You probably think of a logo, a tag line, and the impressions they made on you. It's all in your head! Every car maker makes a vehicle that takes you from point A to point B. That's not their brand. Brand is how you FEEL about the ride. It's about the impressions they create in your mind. Every instructional designer does the same thing. Believe me, after looking at resume after resume, we're using mostly the same tools, we're following the same processes, we're producing the same type of output. So, what makes your brand stand out?

Here are five things you can do to make your personal brand shape that impression!

MOTTO: *Create and share value that both you and others appreciate.*

CULTIVATE it! *Everyone has a personal brand. Whether you are aware of it or not, your energy footprint is out there. I like to use the verb CULTIVATE, as opposed to create or build, because it takes time and effort to grow your brand, just like a garden. If you don't cultivate it, you rely on the beauty of weeds.*

AUDIT your brand before you build a vision! *Personal brand is a living garden. It has seasons, and over time your vision for the garden will change. But before you start planting, you need to audit the impression you've already made. Google your name. See what comes up on your digital footprint. Be mindful what you share and post online. Ask your colleagues, anonymously if you wish, what words they would use to describe you and your work. That's your impression footprint. Your impression might not be the brand you think you are!*

FIND inspirations! *Who are the people that inspire you most? Find them. Connect with them. Be social. Tweet. LinkedIn or meet in real life. Follow them to see what they see. Being associated with people you admire makes your brand stronger as well. It does not mean you should mimic them! Working out loud is a powerful way to share your values and learn from others.*

BE authentic! *Do not cultivate something you don't like. There's nothing more devastating to personal branding than the impression of being fake. You should have a vision and stretch goals where you'd want to be, but be yourself! For example, I was often told in the corporate world that humor might damage my personal brand, because it is perceived as representing someone who is not seriously focused. I accepted that, but that's who I am. I was also told my video clips I made on my YouTube channel are whimsical.*

Whimsical I am then. Your brand may change over time, but stick to your core values.

Reinvent! As I mentioned, your brand is not set in stone. It's a living garden. You and the world around you keep changing. It's okay to reinvent time to time. Create a personal website. Blog, curate, share. Create value for others.

BONUS TIP: Create a logo, tagline, and a short ad about who you are! Hang it up as a poster so you can see it. Every. Single. Day.

The bad news is that everything you do, say, don't do, and don't say shapes your personal brand, both digital and IRL. The good news is that everything you do, say, don't do, and don't say shapes your personal brand, both digital and IRL. Take charge now!

Whimsically,
Rabbit O'Reg

Someone whistles. LI DOE looks around, searching for the source of the noise. Pop! Somebody opened Champagne? LI DOE checks the map on the back of the shield. Just then the White Queen appears from the woods.

White Queen: "Quick! Follow me!"

MENTAL TRAVEL: All through my life
(In which we find out the secret of followers and the truth about lollipops.)

Follow the Leader is a children's game. One person, the leader, is in front of the line. Everyone else lines up behind. Each follower must mimic whatever the leader does in front. If someone can't follow a move, they are out. The last person standing behind the leader wins, and becomes the leader for the next game.

Fun Game, No?

Now, if you're the first person in the line, your view is clear. Everyone else has an obstructed view. The further away you stand from the leader, the more distorted your view. In fact, you might not even see the leader. You see one or maybe two people in front. And those people might not even see the leader either. You see the pattern here? You're not even mimicking the leader! You're mimicking the people in front you, who are mimicking the people in front of them. I'm not talking about corporate culture. Follow the Leader is a children's game, and the point is for the leader to make funky moves that no one can mimic anyway.

Are You a Leader or Follower?

One can argue that social media has changed the definition of "follow" and "lead" in the last decade. You can follow and unfollow anyone you want on Twitter, for example. You're not stuck somewhere in the back row with an obstructed view anymore. You can follow the leader directly. Also, followers are no longer blindly mimicking leaders. In fact, many people follow each other! Nowadays following often means sharing. Sharing ideas, tools, processes, best practices, vision. Following means you get exposure to relevance. In today's digital world, the power is not in hoarding and then distributing information. When a simple search returns billions of bits of information, the power has shifted from accessing to finding relevancy. And that's why you need to follow people you trust. But don't stop there! Follow some of the people they follow.

Your goal of following people might and should be different case by case. Some people you should follow because their vision is so far ahead that you will learn what's coming in the next five years. Clear view of the landscape! Some people you should follow to keep your skillset and tools in shape. They are maybe a year ahead of you. And some people you should follow because they're just plain ahead of you. What tools are they using? What processes are they following? What works today? What mistakes do they make?

And don't stop there! You should also follow some of the people who are following you. Why? Because leader is not a title, it's a status you earn from followers.

That kid in front of the line who does whatever to lose everyone behind and never turns back to look, that is not a leader. That's just a person in front of the line. Unfortunately, we see those people at many companies in leadership positions.

So, next time you see someone in front of the line who acts like "mimic me or you're out," remember: That person is not a leader. That person is just a person in front of the line.

Who's a Leader?

Drew Dudley has a great TED Talk on everyday leadership.[37] He argues that anyone is a leader, even if they're not aware. One of Drew's examples is the Lollipop Moment, where he literally changed someone's mind and life by being somewhere at the right time and in the right moment even without ever realizing it. I'm sure you can recall "Lollipop Moments," where someone's action made a huge difference in your life, yet you probably never told them about it. That person is a leader.

I have a degree in Teaching English as a Foreign Language. The last semester of the program I taught in an elementary school. It was a fun, great group of kids. What they taught me about myself is that teaching is not about "covering the content." It's not even about the classes and homework. It's about engagement, motivation, and inspiration. If kids are motivated and inspired, they'll learn anything. I wasn't there for a semester to deliver lessons; I was there to inspire them enough to be life-long learners of English. What they use the language for is up to them. For example, I introduced them to the script of *The Crow* with Brandon Lee (if you haven't seen the movie, you should). That movie, along with the soundtrack, was not just a story. It turned out to be an inspiration for at least one of the students to pursue English. You never know about the impact of your decision! So, choose them wisely, in case someone decides to follow you.

Who to Follow?

Following the "right people" gives you the advantage of seeing trends, receiving tips and best practices, or just being in the loop. I want to emphasize that "right" probably means something different to you than to me or to others. Based on your current skills, knowledge, expertise, and interest, the list can be extended by many more talented people out there. Here are just some of the people (see compiled lists of people to follow at the bottom).

Instructional Design

Cathy Moore, Michael Allen, Clark Quinn, Ryan Tracey, Tom Kuhlmann, Sharon Boller, Megan Torrance, Christy Tucker, Ryan Martin, Anna Sabramowicz, .

---

37   https://www.ted.com/talks/drew_dudley_everyday_leadership.

Game Thinking (Gamification and Game Design)

Amy Jo Kim, Karl Kapp, Yu-kai Chou, Sharon Boller, Andrew Hughes, Kevin Werbach, Chris Aviles, Frank Lee, An Coppens, Jane McGonigal, Ashley Alicea, Steven Isaacs, Monica Cornetti, David Mullich, Andrzej Marczweski, Margaret Wallace, Nicole Lazzaro, Gabe Zichermann

E-Learning Design and Development

Articulate E-Learning Heroes weekly challenge. This is a must if you're in eLearning design and development. Follow David Anderson (@elearning) for updates and curated example notifications.

Podcasts

Sam Rogers collected a solid list of top podcast resources.[38]

Modern Workplace Learning

Jane Hart, Shannon Tipton, David Kelly, JD Dillon, Laura Overton, Jane Bozarth, Donald H. Taylor, Harold Jarche.

Science of Learning

Will Thalheimer, Patti Shank, Jane Bozarth, Julie Dirksen, Ruth Clark.

Social Learning

Helen Blunden, Michel Ockers, Lisa Minogue-White.

List of Folks to Follow

Brian Washburn put together a good list of L&D professionals.[39] Not sure if social media is for L&D at all? Read Shannon Tipton's blog, *Learning Rebels*:[40]

---

38   http://snapsynapse.com/ultimate-lnd-podcast-guide-2017/

39   https://trainlikeachampion.wordpress.com/2016/04/28/if-youre-not-following-these-18-people-in-order-to-help-hone-your-ld-trade-craft-you-should/.

40   http://learningrebels.com/2016/05/02/3-reasons-trainers-dont-need-social-media/.

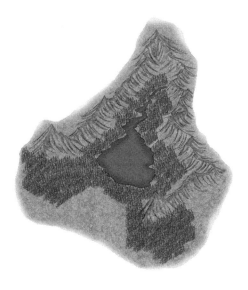

Necklace of Hope

The White Queen is in a hurry. Whatever makes her move fast, good enough reason for LI DOE to follow. They arrive to a spring.

White Queen: "Stay here! Don't move until I come back."

LI DOE: "Why?"

White Queen: "Because you're in the Valley of the Gut Gifted. If any of the dead souls touch you, you become a Carrier."

LI DOE: "Carrier of what?"

White Queen: "Just don't move, whatever happens! Keep this on!"

The White Queen hands over a necklace made out of shiny beads that reflect the bright Sun.

Oh, the Valley of the Gut Gifted. It is packed with good-intentioned humans who trust their guts instead of research and evidence. These humans, sometimes unknowingly, are Carriers of ghosts. Ghosts of myths buried in the Myth Bunkers. The fresh water lake in the middle of the Valley, called April Fools, triggers all sorts of funny ideas in the brain. Traditionally, once a year, on April 1, humans are allowed a sip of its water and make practical jokes about each other. Other days, fishing and drinking are strictly prohibited to protect the living from myths. What about treatment for Carriers? Someone said, in today's world April Fools' is the only day when humans mistrust what they read on the internet. Treat every day like April Fools' day! Always check your sources!

IRL CHALLENGES:

1. Go underground in your organization and map out communities (either sanctioned or undercover). Find active members and organizers, their tools, methods, etc. Build a bridge between them.

2. Organize "Show and Tell" launches. Something like a TED talk but TED lunch. Have people share what they're working on. The more cross-functional you can make it the better.

3. Whatever you do, please don't start writing manifestos, charters, and SOPs (standard operating procedures) for the collaboration committee! Start small, be nimble, rely on those who are already sharing.

4. Show Your Work! Share not only what you did but how you did with others. HOW = HELP OTHERS WIN

5. See what's Jane Bozarth is up to.

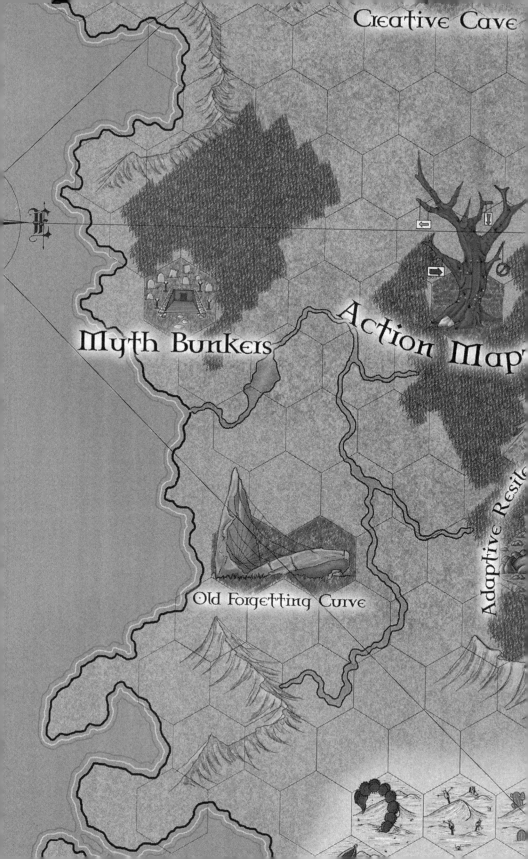

Chapter Seven

MYTH (DE)BUNKING
(FROM LEARNING MYTHS TO THE
WORKPLACE REAL THINGS)

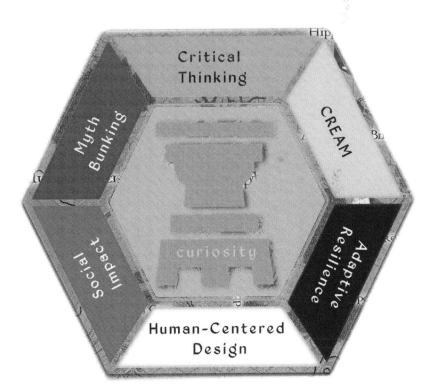

Pursuit of Trait 6/6: Myth Bunking

Where Are We?

Myth Bunkers is the resting place of the WORL&D. Many theories, fake ideas, and misconceptions are resting underground here peacefully. While it is a haunted place with only an entrance (those who enter give up all myth), from time to time there are resurrections when the Red King's mercenaries dig up old souls in the graveyard. Fortunately, the community has set up vigilance researchers to spot and capture the myths should they resurrect. Old fairy tales often refer to a secret passage between the Myth Bunkers and the forbidden lake in the Valley of the Gut Gifted. An ancient curse says: if a traveler spends too much time crossing the Valley of the Gut Gifted, a buried ghost might entice the traveler, who then becomes the Carrier. And that's how myths spread. If you see one, speak up!

LI DOE follows his curiosity to find the source of a humming sound among the tombstones of learning myths when the White Queen grabs him.

White Queen: "Come with me!"

LI DOE: "Where?"

White Queen: "Actionmap Town. Quick!"

Actionmap Town was founded by the Moore family. The Moores possessed good analytical thinking. Originally, they were hunters. The best Bore hunters in the world. When the O'Rious brothers settled here, the WORL&D was full of bores. Bores, living in their Boredom, were wild animals. They were feared across the land. The Bores slowly lulled their prey to sleep, and gradually poisoned their minds. Bores could hunt both face to face and online. When a human got bit by a Bore, their performance suffered. The Moores took on the challenge to effectively fight all Bores in the their infinite Boredom. Throughout several generations, the Moores evolved their techniques and formalized their approach. They built the Dunes of Obstacalities in the South to protect the land. Eventually, they settled in a branching tree with deep roots in effective training soil. They named their tree Actionmap Town.

The White Queen drags LI DOE all the way to the trunk of the main tree. She gives LI DOE a necklace.

White Queen: "Hang out here with this necklace at the tree, and don't move!"

LI DOE: "Don't move? Until when?"

White Queen: "Until I return with instructions. Don't move!"

And off she hurries. LI DOE senses the urgency in the White Queen's voice, but that doesn't stop him from checking out something that looks interesting in the distance: Dunes of Obstacalities.

Examples of Asking the Right Questions

I have to confess. I hate driving. My limit is probably two hours. I don't like cars either. Yes, they look charming in the commercials sliding along the ocean in a closed road where there's no traffic. But you pay insurance; you get depressed by the first scratch; they guzzle gasoline. I don't know, it's just not my thing. But driving has given me two a-ha moments in terms of learning.

I didn't have to drive until I was like twenty-nine. In Hungary, getting a driver's license is like earning a college degree. First, you must take a mandatory traffic rules knowledge course. It lasts weeks. You must pass three tests: one on the rules of the road (and by that I mean things like "fifteen cars turning into an intersection when a trolley is signaling left to overtake a bus" kinds of situations), one on how the engine works, and one on first aid.

The "rules of the road" book is as thick as the phone book used to be. So, by the time you get all this done, you pretty much know everything, I repeat, EVERYTHING, about cars, people, and traffic. What you don't know is how to drive.

And that's why you must sign up for fifty hours of mandatory hands-on driving with a qualified instructor. Now, you don't just go out in the street and drive! No, no! First, you must pass the technical exam in a closed course. You must be able to parallel park, back into a tight spot, 180, 360, whatever life might bring on you.

Once, you pass that, THEN you must drive in traffic with the instructor. Both in daylight and at night. You develop a very intimate relationship with your instructor. Hours and hours spent together in traffic, learning the ins and outs of driving. It often feels like the journey of a young Jedi preparing for the final encounter with the Death Star.

My first a-ha moment was the very moment I met my qualified instructor.

MENTAL TRAVEL: Hungary, 1999
(Where the curse begins.)

Again, at this point I KNOW everything about cars, engines, and health. Except I've never once driven car. Let's call my instructor Laszlo. Laszlo opens the car door and tells me to sit and drive while he's in the passenger's seat. Another learner, let's call her Anita, is sitting in the back.

I tell Laszlo that I don't know how to drive, which is kind of the reason I'm here. Laszlo gets visibly frustrated, starts naming every little thing on the dashboard: here's the gas, mileage, radio, etc. And that's when my moment happens. To save his speech, I interrupt Laszlo and reiterate: I KNOW what these things are; I DID pass that exam. What I don't know is how to drive.

Now, that pushes Laszlo's button. Laszlo releases the hand break, turns on the ignition, and screams: YOU KNOW EVERYTHING? GO! That moment I realize he has no idea of the difference between knowledge and skill. I must also remind you that learning on a twenty-year-old Russian manual car that "has a soul" is not the easiest job. If you release the clutch too fast, you hurt its soul, and the engine hops and dies. If you release it too slowly, it spins like James Bond. Either way, you'll get yelled at.

I don't know why I didn't change instructors. I think I blamed myself for not being able to drive at the age of twenty-nine. Eventually, I passed the exam and got my driver's license. I contemplated asking for a refund, but then I realized the lesson I had received as a lifelong learner wasn't about driving, it was about teaching. It was about knowledge, skills, and attitude. And those lessons were worth the money.

Today, I know my instructor was suffering from the Curse of Knowledge. Subject matter experts, who are too close to the content and know so much about the subject, often suffer from the Curse of Knowledge. Under the Curse of Knowledge, people have a hard time imagining themselves in a new learner's position. They often lump instructions together and forget tiny yet crucial details. Like when the first time we were in the streets and Laszlo said, "Just look way ahead on the road. Ignore the car."

Sure you could do that, Laszlo, because YOU don't need to worry about the car. But I wasn't there yet.

How do you deal with the Curse of Knowledge? One suggestion is to playtest your instructions on end users. Find someone who's your target audience and watch them go through the steps. Tell them to explain their thinking as they go through the material. Tell them to verbalize what questions they have, what decisions they're making. You will learn a lot from the experience.

MENTAL TRAVEL: Massachusetts, 2000
(Where the curse continues.)

The second driving a-ha moment comes in the States. I have an international driver's license, so have to take the U.S. version of the exam. When I look at the "book" with the rules of the road to memorize, I think it is a joke. It is thinner than one chapter on turning left in the Hungarian hundred-page version. Also, half the book is about what happens when you drive under the influence, won't pay the fine, don't showing up in court, etc. All that I skip, since in Hungary there's zero tolerance on drinking and driving anyway.

I go to the DMV to take the exam. I see people coming in, literally asking what they need to do to get a driver's license, and then just flipping through the book right there. No study. Nothing. So, what can go wrong for me, right? Seventy dollars for a ten-minute quiz! That's what could go wrong. In the Hungarian exam, we had to answer over a hundred questions. This time I had only twenty. Piece of cake. And I failed.

Dude, I got like eight questions incorrect!!! That was my a-ha moment #2. I failed because I didn't study all the crap that can happen to you when you break the law. Meanwhile, this woman turns to me while taking the test and asks me, I kid you not, whether she can turn left if there are two yellow lines in the middle of the road. She passed.

I never in my life felt like more of a loser. I blew seventy dollars, but, more important, I was angry with the system. A system that is designed not to provide positive feedback on how to DO things, but rather to test on what happens when you fail to do them and so break the law. (I passed the next day.)

My mistake was not asking the right questions in the first place. I should have asked what the business goal was for the test? Is it to let people who know the basic rules drive in public? People who can read signs? And cause less accidents? Or is to make sure everyone understands the consequences WHEN they break the law? These are two very different approaches.

The first I call the *Law & Order* approach. The second is the TSA approach. The *Law & Order* approach assumes innocence until proven guilty in a court of law. That means everyone assumes you're going to follow the rules, and the exam serves as a reassurance that you know the rules.

The TSA approach is the "guilty until proven innocent" approach. TSA agents at the airport make you stand in line and go through a metal detector. Everyone in line is suspicious, and everyone has to prove their innocence. The TSA approach assumes you're going to break the law, therefore, they want you to know what the consequences are.

Adding five questions to the end of a course as a COL (confirmation of learning) is the TSA approach. I assume you're not learning anything here, and if there wasn't any consequences, you would probably not even open this course. It's a punishment. Oh, but that's how you prove you learned, right? Well, recalling mostly facts from your short-term memory right after taking a course has little to do with learning in the long run. Sorry to break the news for all you compliance-watchers.

What if your system would congratulate learners on finishing the course, and inform you that in eight days you'll receive an invitation to answer five questions based on what you learned today? At least the recall would be better. Performance, who knows? What if your supervisor or manager would get a notification and they would be asked to OBSERVE the desired performance? Now that would make humans think twice about not paying attention. :)

LI DOE doesn't feel good. His head is spinning, his neurons are filled with stuff. His neural network is overloaded. The dark cell he's sitting in is empty. Only a window with iron bars provides some light. Someone throws a necklace in.

White Queen: "Put this on."

LI DOE: "What's this?"

White Queen: "Necklace of Hope. When they start glowing, spin around the cell as fast as you can and focus on the Red King."

LI DOE: "What happened? Where am I?"

White Queen: "You're on the island of Cognitive Overlord. It's our prison. You can only leave if you clear the clutter in your mind."

LI DOE: "How come I'm here when I didn't even know this place existed?"

White Queen: "The Red King found you a threat. He overloaded your cognitive functions. You've split into multiple instances. I'll find the others."

LI DOE: "Threat? What threat? I just want to go home."

Bigger Than Y2K?

Let me ask this! In the year 2000, what was the biggest threat to the United States?

No, not Y2K. No, not the fact that the U.S. population tops 282 million. A rise in mad cow disease? Too far ... Ian Thorpe? Getting closer ... Texas Governor George W. Bush defeating Vice President Al Gore? The case of the hanging chads? No, something much more dangerous was happening under the radar. And guess what, it has to do with eLearning.

Here's how the story unfolds: I am a full-time fiancé in 2000, living in Cambridge. To get the ball rolling with my citizenship, we start the paperwork at the INS (now the Department of Homeland Security). Imagine a giant waiting room, filled with people. Waiting. In the middle of the room, way up in the ceiling, attached to a pillar, is a television. Again, this is year 2000. No Facebook, iPhone, Twitter, or any of that nonsense ... Pure waiting.

This TV is chained to the pillar, I guess because otherwise someone might somehow, somewhere, find a ladder to climb up to steal it, or something. Anyway, that's not what the threat is about. The TV is on, pretty loud. The bottom part of the TV is secured with scotch tape. There's no remote control anywhere, but in case someone finds a way to climb up to the chained TV they would be able to adjust the volume, OR ...

And we're getting closer to the biggest threat in the country: CHANGE THE CHANNEL!! Imagine what happens if you hand over the control to people to change the channel!

This is a fact. In the year 2000, the biggest threat immigrants were posing to the United States was having the ability to change the channel.

Now, here comes my question. Conjure the image of this securely chained, scotch-taped, inaccessible TV blaring in the waiting room all day ... What channel do you think it was set to?

Tweet me your guess before you find the answer later: @rabbitoreg #WhoIsLiDoe.

What channel did you guess? News? Weather? Sports? Music? Wrong.

The CHANNEL GUIDE!!

I can't think of a more ironic way of introducing the Land of the Free than showing all the channels you could see IF you had access to the TV. Because in 2000, the Channel Guide was not the sexiest thing, believe me. Of course, we're not talking national threat here. We're talking about eLearning.

Have you ever had the same feeling while taking an eLearning course? That you are the biggest threat? So the content has to be securely chained to the menu? Where you have no control over what you see or how you proceed? Where you have to wait for the Next button to show up? But it won't, until the voiceover stops blabbing!! Yet you secretly hope there's a bug in the system and you can skip it? That you feel like even just a remote control would at least make you feel a tiny little bit more engaged?

Do you think whoever made the decision to chain and scotch-tape that TV had to sit and watch it all day? Same thing happens to eLearning courses. Often, people in charge make decisions about how and what others will learn. From their perspective, it's the content that counts. Like showing the Channel Guide would give the same experience as watching a show? Always think USER EXPERIENCE. Think in ACTIONS, not content. Think what happens BEFORE, DURING, and AFTER the course. There's a difference between guiding the learner through the experience and force-feeding through the content.

Next time leadership complains about employee engagement, and asks you to create a leadership video with slides over slides of blah-blah, with a Next button that you have to wait for ...

... do this instead: ask them to go home, chain their TV set, scotch-tape the bottom part, crank up the volume, turn it to the guide, and throw away the batteries from the remote. Then, bring in a random beloved family member to sit there and watch. This is a prime example of why eLearning has its bad reputation. Speaking of prime!

Priming

Remember the Truth-Tellers and Liars challenge? About the two ant tribes living on the stump? You had to come up with one question to find out how to get to the Truth-Tellers Colony. Let's see if you can solve this version:

"Imagine an island where everyone is a Truth-Teller or Liar. Truth-Tellers always tell the truth when asked; Liars always lie when asked a question. I want to go the Truth-Tellers Village. On the road, I arrive to a fork. One road leads to the Truth-Tellers Village; the other to the Liars Village. A person is standing there but I'm not sure whether that person is a Truth-Teller or a Liar.

Me: "Are you a Liar?"

Person: "Yes."

Given that exchange, do I know which way to go to the Truth-Tellers Village? No, I don't.

Was that person a Liar or a Truth-Teller?

Your mind may spin on this one for a while. If the person is Truth-Teller, he or she wouldn't say yes to the question: Are you a Liar? Okay, then the person is a Liar. But if the person is a Liar, he or she wouldn't say yes to the question either. So, the person is neither a Truth-Teller nor a Liar. But everyone on the island is either a Truth-Teller or a Liar. *Hmmm* ... paradox?

If you're confused, it's probably because of your mind. When I asked if you remember the challenge previously, it was intentional, to give you details to recall the original story. When I reminded you of the Truth-Teller story, your brain automatically filled the gaps in the new challenge, based on your prior knowledge. But there's a difference between the two stories.

When I said "everyone is a Truth-Teller or a Liar," I said EVERYONE on the island.

Then ...

"... I arrive to a fork." If I arrive to a fork on the island, AM I ON THE ISLAND? Yes. And if "everyone" on the island is either a Truth-Teller or a Liar, I'm one of them. This adds another layer of complexity to the story, because now it's not just the answers you're looking at but the narrator's response as well. Now, if I'm a Truth-Teller, the story doesn't have a resolution. Why? Because neither a Truth-Teller nor a Liar would answer with yes to the first question. But if I am a Liar, the answer I received was not a yes but a no. And if the answer is a no, that person could be either a Truth-Teller or a Liar. Both would say no. I also stated that I don't know which way to go to the Truth-Tellers Village. Since I'm a Liar, my real answer is yes, I know which way to go. How? Because I'm a Liar. I know which way I live. I just have to go the opposite way.

All in all, this whole conversation didn't make a difference. If I live on the island, I know where the Truth-Tellers Village is, so this whole conversation was a waste of time. I could've just ignored that person and walk past.

In L&D, we often assume that showing a storyboard (document with text and mockups and descriptions of what happens on the screen) is a sure way to get approval for the eLearning project. Then the surprise comes in the middle of the project, when the stakeholders see the module for the first time. That's not what they wanted. How come? They approved it! It was clearly stated how a bubble will pop from the character's head with the scenario. Our brain uses imagination to fill the gap when information is missing. How stakeholders see the experience in their mind's eye might be completely different from what you put down in the storyboard. The brain does funky things we are not even aware of. Like priming.

In *Thinking Fast and Slow*, Daniel Kahneman spends a chapter on priming. Priming effect seems fascinating. It allows you to manipulate people without their knowledge. Imagine the marketing power of the priming science when showing words or colors would make young kids run out and buy stuff!! Like throwing "Buy Pepsi" on the screen in a commercial on just enough frames that your conscious brain doesn't even notice it, but your unconscious does.

In *Thinking Fast and Slow*, I found the "Florida Effect" to be one of the most fascinating examples of priming. In this experiment, researchers gave words to people to put a sentence together, and then sent them to the second room at the end of a long hallway. Now, half the group got words associated with being old; the others got words associated with being young.

The experiment, however, wasn't so much about the sentences they put together. They measured the time it takes for the participants to reach the second room. And guess what! The group that had words associated with being old took significantly longer to reach the second room. They walked slowly! Like old people!

I also found a fascinating statistical analysis on the published studies that show that the priming effect demonstrated in Daniel Kahneman's book might not be as significant as it seems.[41] In fact, most of the studies could not be replicated later on to bring the same results. Therefore, based on the calculated R-index (replicability index), the authors of the article conclude the following regarding the priming effect:

"[R]eaders of *Thinking Fast and Slow* should be skeptical about the reported results and they should disregard Kahneman's statement that 'you have no choice but to accept that the major conclusions of these studies are true.' Our analysis actually leads to the opposite conclusion. 'You should not accept any of the conclusions of these studies as true.'"

So next time someone tells you that just keeping a pencil in your mouth (smile) will make you find cartoons funnier, while keeping a pencil

---

41   https://replicationindex.wordpress.com/category/
thinking-fast-and-slow/.

between your lips and nose (frown) less funny, just ask them about the replicability of these findings. Do you research before you accidentally become a Carrier of myth? For example, the debunked theory of learning styles (matching someone's "learning style" with that of the same instructional style leads to more effective learning) is still out there because of accidental Carriers. Do your research! Check your sources!

The Fox Research Trap

A quick Google research reveals the answer to the question: what does the fox say?

Now, this might be obvious for you, but the fox says *ding-ding-ding-ding-dingerigeding*. I'm sure someone has already created a one-page infographic on this. If you're not sure about this fact, check out one of the top-watched videos on YouTube in 2013 by Ylvis. The "What Does the Fox Say" became the highest-ranked song by a Norwegian artist since A-ha released "Take On Me" in 1985. The WORL&D has changed.

MENTAL TRAVEL: Robot Technics, 1993
(Where we learn about the importance of robots.)

At college, we had a class called Robot Technics. It was a ton of math and graphs about how and what robotic arms can do. Luckily, there was a guy in the group who was smart enough to understand AND take good notes. So, when the exam came, we all copied his notes to learn. It kind of worked out. Until one day we fell into the above mentioned "Fox Research Trap."

The professor comes in with the exam papers and looks around suspiciously. He says everyone passed but someone must explain this mystery: what's in the robot's hand?

Nobody has a clue what the prof is talking about. He goes: everyone but one person drew this THING in the robot's hand that has nothing to do with robot technics. I don't know what it is. It looks like a handgun!

And the smart guy bursts out laughing ... Turns out, he was bored during the lesson and drew a handgun in the robot's hand. We all copied his notes as is, never questioning a pixel on that graph. Now, he knew it didn't belong there, so he didn't equip the robot with a handgun, while we all did.

Lessons learned: Know your data! Do your research! A single-page infographic posted on social media is tempting. Especially if it makes sense. But make sure you know where it comes from. Check out the *Will at Work Learning* blog, for example, to bust some of the myths out there. Use Google Scholar and read up on your topic. Many times, studies that end up an infographic have been conducted by vendors (selling the very product the results indicate you should have).

We see what we want to see. Another social media example is an infographic showing the top seven game mechanics that work best. After digging into the source, it turns out it was a survey (no sample size) conducted on user preferences on some sites, where half the participants didn't even visit the sites. So, the findings were right: within those users who visited the sites in question, they did prefer some of the gamification techniques over others. But that's different from a one-pager stating the seven game mechanics that work best in general! In other words, just because you asked your neighbor about their favorite pizza places, doesn't mean those are the top ones in the country.

Finding information is very easy nowadays. Like searching for what the fox says. Making sense of the received data starts with asking fundamental critical questions. Is it really ding-ding-ding-ding-dingerigeding?

Do your homework, do your research! You can easily become a Carrier just by liking or sharing something on social media that "makes sense." It's okay to believe in your opinions, but it's better to back them up with research.

IRL CHALLENGES:

1. Join the debunker club to stop the myth!![42]

---

42   http://www.debunker.club/

Hippo Campus
Amyg D'la Bridge
Maptown
Training
Rabbit O'Reg
Adaptive Resilence
Scope Creep Creek
Obstacalities

Chapter Eight

REFLECTION, REFLECTION, REFLECTION

You may see your reflection in the Scope Creep Creek, a man-made outdoor swimming pool, any time. It has a zero entry point on one end. Don't get fooled! If you're not paying attention, you find yourself in deep water very soon. You learn to swim by treading water here. You'll find the best swim coaches in the deep end.

```
EXT. SCOPE CREEP CREEK SWIMMING POOL --
DAY

A hands-on SWIM COACH stands in the pool,
helping kids practicing the right moves. A
MOTHER drags along his skinny TEENAGE SON
to the pool. She keeps her distance from
any splash.

                    MOTHER
          Are you the coach?

                  SWIM COACH
          Yes, M'am. I am.
```

                    MOTHER
          Good! So, you're an
          expert at how to teach
          kids to swim?

                SWIM COACH
          I'm doing my best...

                    MOTHER
          I need my son to learn
          how to swim.

                SWIM COACH
          Perfect place to be.
     (to the Son, smiling)
          Hi, I'm Coach. What's
          your name?

                  MOTHER
          Do you know need to
          know his name in order
          to teach him to swim?

                SWIM COACH
          Well, I usually like
          to know a little bit
          about my audience...

                  MOTHER
          Elmo!

                SWIM COACH
          Elmo is his name?

                    MOTHER
No. Elmo stands for:
enough, let's move on!
How long does it take
usually? To learn to
swim?

                SWIM COACH
It depends how you
measure...

                    MOTHER
You don't seem to
be an expert at this
thing.

                SWIM COACH
It depends on prior
skills and...

                    MOTHER
Not even a bath.

                SWIM COACH
No problem. Usually,
twice a week, for
four weeks is a good
base...

                    MOTHER
No, no, no! We're
going on a river
cruise, and he needs
to be able to swim by
then.

                    SWIM COACH
          Okay. When is the
          trip?

                    MOTHER
          We're actually on the
          way there. I heard
          about this thing:
          microlearning. Can
          you do that for 15
          minutes?

                    SWIM COACH
          Wow. Then let's hop
          in and maybe we can
          work on some survival
          basics?

                    MOTHER
          Hop in where?

                    SWIM COACH
          Into the water.

                    MOTHER
          No, no, no! I don't
          want him to get wet.

                    SWIM COACH
          Then how do you want
          me to teach him to
          swim?

MOTHER
It feels like I'm not
getting the value for
my money here. I was
thinking of a show-
me, test-me micro
approach. You would
swim a couple of laps,
commenting on what
you're doing, and then
my son would answer
5 multiple choice
questions. Or do you
have a free tip-sheet?
Only if laminated!

LI DOE's attention suddenly shifts from the swimming pool to a noise behind him. From the woods a Red Fox faces him eye to eye.

LI DOE: "What's going on?"

The Fox snarls at LI DOE first, then starts humming a tune.

LI DOE: "Oh, you must be an auditory vark."

LI DOE is confused. Where did he hear this tune before? Three more Red Foxes join the humming. The four beasts step closer to LI DOE.

LI DOE: "What the fox? Four Non Blondes?"

LI DOE picks up a branch from the ground, check his swings, bends his knees, and signals for the pitch.

MENTAL TRAVEL: Cambridge, 2000
(Where I work as a full-time fiancé.)

When I moved to Cambridge as a full-time fiancé, I had four months before our wedding. I couldn't sit still without learning. My fiancée was finishing up her Ed.D. studies, so I had some free time to explore the new world. First, I took on baseball. I had never played or watched baseball before. I watched the first game of the season, alone in the apartment. Now, watching baseball for the first time is not the most intuitive exercise. Over Spring Break, I "picked" my favorite player, the only one whose name I could remember from the short clip. Well, I picked this guy who was a backup pitcher, Wakefield. He had played like zilch games, because when I dropped into the Red Sox season Pedro Martinez was dominating the series.

Back to my learning. I was confused by how sometimes they run, sometimes they don't, even after hitting the ball. And sometimes, without even hitting, they run. Then there was this thing where they intentionally move someone to first base. It was a long lesson. The Red Sox lost that day. When my fiancée came home from the meeting I was excited to report out what I had learned, and asked what this loss mean for the Red Sox. She said nothing. There's going to be hundreds of games to come.

Like any lifelong learner, I quickly picked up the rules of baseball. But that wasn't enough to make me a fan. I needed to know the ins and outs of the team. So, I signed for a class at the Cambridge Adult Learning Center. The "How to Become a Red Sox Fan?" course was incredible.

It was the most bizarre learning experience. On one hand, we had people who didn't know a thing about baseball, much less the Red Sox. On the other hand, we had guys discussing the pros and cons of left-handed pitchers versus right-handed hitters, citing stats all over. I don't remember a thing from the course except "The Curse of the Bambino" and Babe Ruth. That somehow came up in every class.

I am now highly trained to be Red Sox fan, even if living in Philly.

After I left Cambridge, the curse was lifted. That reminds me of another curse. Apparently, when some chump developer in Philly broke the unwritten law disallowing buildings taller than the *William Penn* statue atop Philadelphia City Hall, the Red King put a curse on the city: "No major sports titles to be won here." And there weren't any. Until I came here. In both places, I managed to break the curse. I think this superpower comes from my early days of bringing down a Communist regime. If anyone has a long curse to break, just let me know!

Taking a Chance

If you had ten chances to roll a dice, would you rather be guaranteed $5 for every roll ($50 total), or risk winning $100, but only if you roll at least one six?

In 2016 I was speaking at the ATD TechKnowledge conference in Las Vegas. After a long day of "conferencing," I tried my luck on a machine. A one-cent machine. I was curious how these machines can make you voluntarily throw away so much money for nothing in return (well, you get a free beer or something if you have time to wait for the slow service).

Here's how it works! You put a dollar in. That is 100 cents. Now, the machine is not counting in cents. It counts in points! You start with like 1,000 points. Each time you roll, the minimum you bet is one cent. That's 100 points. You now have only 900 points. But all the whistles and bells go on as the counter shows that you've just won 50 points!!! You're on a roll here. You raise the bet to 50 cents (500 points). You win again! This time 300 points!!!

In reality, you put in 100 cents initially, and now you only have 75 cents. But you FEEL like you're on a winning streak. The coin machines are nothing but masters of storytelling. They're so good at telling a good story that you never notice reality around you. They're banking on the thrill of risk. Risk is a powerful game mechanic. Risk always includes choice. Without choice, you don't buy in. The choice may be loaded, but still there's choice. And with choice, there's chance. The chance is the reward. Not what you win. The excitement of the possibility is what boils your blood, not the actual reward. It pumps so much adrenalin in your brain that you buy this story big-time. The question is, are you there to win? Or are you there for entertainment?

I'm not a huge gambler, but based on stats, I'd probably suggest playing Black Jack over playing a machine that tells you a good story about winning while eating up your money.

As for L&D, whenever you can, sneak in some risk in the learning experience. A balanced risk involves choice, chance, and rewards. If these align with your performance goals, you can be the coin machine that tells an exciting story. You don't need to think in high-roller's terms. At eLearning Guild's DevLearn Conference I showed an xAPI example, where teams answered a question as well as showed their confidence in a slider. If the answer was correct, the team received points based on their indicated confidence. If they were 100 percent confident, they received the 100 percent of the maximum points. If they were just 80 percent, they only got 80 percent of the maximum points. Where's the risk in this? Well, if they didn't choose the right answer and they were 80 percent confident in their wrong answer, they lost 80 percent of the maximum points.

MENTAL TRAVEL: Hungary, 1989
(Where I "meet" the President of the United States.)

It was the summer of 1989. The Iron Curtain is falling down with the first democratic elections looming over the Communist Party. Meanwhile, I have just graduated from high school. When the news comes that President Bush is stopping by Budapest as the first "Free World" leader to say hi to the birth of a new generation, I know I have to be there.

Kossuth Square, in Budapest, is packed six hours before the designated time for the speech. We are all young, energetic, and enthusiastic. The exact kind of crowd that politicians thrive on. First, President Bush is late. Things go downhill from there ...

A summer storm appears out of nowhere. The crowd is inside the security parameters, so there's nowhere to go. We get drenched. Everyone is soaking wet. But we don't care. There's always a silver lining. I get the front row, right at the stage.

Finally, President Bush arrives. Some drizzling rain is still hesitantly falling, but I guess a PR person must have told President Bush that maybe he should ditch the umbrella, as everyone in the audience is soaking wet. He does. We cheer.

Then, completely unexpectedly (or carefully orchestrated?), he says something like he's going to tear his speech apart and speak from the heart. Now that gets a lot of cheers. Not from the translator. She is struggling to keep up from that moment on.

The speech is short and sweet and I don't remember a thing. I don't really trust politicians. I think it was about a promising, bright future or something. But what happens after, in my immediate future, is not so bright.

Since the President is late, I miss the train I am supposed to take home. Also, to get to the train station, first you have to take the subway. Have you ever tried going down there against that cold draft when you're soaking wet? It's freezing.

Then more bad news for me (Hungary, in contrast, is hunky-dory). The last train isn't going to take me home. I have to change at Kál-Kápolna. Yes, Kál-Kápolna is as bad as it sounds. On the train, I find some newspapers and put them in between my wet clothes and my body. They warm me up. Journalism has been close to my heart ever since.

Back to Kál-Kápolna. At midnight, I get off the train. It is pitch dark, not a soul around. I wake up a clerk inside and ask when my next connection is. At 5 a.m. I look around, grab some chairs in an empty waiting room, and lie down for the next excruciatingly long five hours. Me, my newspaper, and the chairs. Every time someone moves, coughs, mumbles I open my eyes. Remember, this was before cellphones and internet! In Kál-Kápolna.

In retrospect, I can say that President Bush's first move in Hungary was to force me to sleep in the Kál-Kápolna train station, on three chairs, soaking wet but filled with hope for a better, brighter future. Little did I know that later I would be a U.S. citizen, voting in an election that would bring the first African American President into the White House. President Obama never once forced me to sleep in a train station.

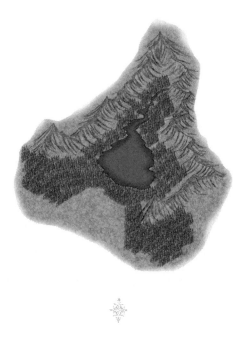

In the Valley of the Gut Gifted LI DOE stares at her reflection in the forbidden lake. What he sees is clearly confusing. It doesn't look like the LI DOE she knows. It looks like a White Queen. And the reflection is clearly humming a tune. LI DOE finds it mesmerizing. He's is about to touch the reflection, when ...

White Queen: "Stop!"

LI DOE freezes.

White Queen: "If your mind become a Carrier, you won't be able to reunite with your other selves."

LI DOE: "Other selves?"

White Queen: "Keep this necklace on! There's Red Foxes all over. When the necklace starts to glow, I want you to spin around as fast as you can, focusing on one thing: the Red King. I will tell the other LI DOEs the same. If you all spin at the same time, focusing on the same thing, you will reunite for the fight. If not, you will have no chance. Your spinning will literally be the difference between dead or alive."

Spinning a name: rabbitoreg

Rabbit O'Reg is not what it seems. Some say it's an Old Rabbit, some say it's a Horse. Either way, Rabbit O'Reg is the source of whimsicality in the WORL&D. Humans often visit Rabbit O'Reg with questions about the history and the future of L&D. As if Rabbit O'Reg had any answers.

The answer is always a question, the same question:

"Are you asking the right questions?"

Why rabbitoreg.com?

My blog and my Twitter handle are "rabbitoreg." I'm sure it's a contender for the Worst Names for Marketing Award. But there's a reason I keep it. I'm originally from Hungary, but I've spent most of my professional life in the States. Therefore, my personal brand, rabbitoreg, reflects the dual nationality. Rabbit is the American part. Oreg (*öreg*) is "old" in Hungarian. The two words together, "old rabbit" in Hunglish, represent who I am and how I think. In fact, this was my very first blog on rabbitoreg.com years ago:

Feeling Like a Lonely Grasshopper?

Let's face it. We've all been there. Your funny status on Facebook, the hilarious picture on Instagram, the wittiest restaurant review blog on WordPress, your hit song on YouTube, or maybe your most uncanny 150 characters ever in the alphabet on Twitter. And yet, now beyond legal drinking age, you still have not gone viral. And that makes you feel like a lonely grasshopper in the woods.

You say you don't care about the viral thing? Then why do you count the "likes" meticulously after each comment? Cause sooner or later, it happens. The virtual failure interferes with your reality. Start questioning yourself at work? At home? Am I not funny enough? Do I not have what it takes to go viral when a grumpy cat can do it? Or a golden dress? Why don't my friends share my posts? Do I still have friends? At that point, you're on the slippery slope of what we call viral anxiety.

You lose interest even in Pinterest, become jealous of your friends' lives (I mean posts), and yes, you know who you are, grab a glass of alcohol in the saddest happy hour ever with some co-workers you, by the way, totally despise otherwise.

Good news! You're not the only one. Let me tell you about Rabbitoreg. Rabbitoreg is the fictitious name of a real horse. And by real I mean I made it from Play-Doh. When my daughter is about two, we buy Play-Doh to introduce her to the magical world of unbridled creativity. Filled with enthusiasm, I make a horse to show how this magic manifests in the hands of the trained expert she too can be with practice. I hand over my beautiful horse to her, with these bittersweet parting words: "Look, you can make anything from Play-Doh!" I am sure this moment will definitely go viral.

This is what actually happens: the horse triggers the biggest smile. While admiring my expert creation, my daughter turns to me with the most innocent praise on her face:

"Daddy! Wow! You made an old rabbit?"

I branded myself Rabbitoreg in retrospect. Whether it goes viral or just makes one person smile, ultimately, it's nothing but Play-Doh. That's all it is. Play-Doh. People matter; the rest, is just Play-Doh. Be smart out there, folks! Thanks for reading this!

MENTAL TRAVEL: Pondering the Past, 2014ish (Where I "sample" Suzanne Vega in Tom's Diner)

I am driving on the highway with my teenage daughter. When you have a teenage daughter, you're forced to listen to their music. That's a rule. On two occasions (years apart), I recognize the original song "sampled." And say: "That's A-ha" / "That's Suzanne Vega." And I was ready to head down memory lane to share all the fond memories the songs conjure in my head. But my daughter's look stops me. She had no idea about A-ha and Suzanne Vega. She was listening to a new hit.

And being a teenager, she shrugged: "Dad, I'm more into the future than pondering the past."

"Pondering the Past?"

That made me think about how we design learning. Are we preoccupied with pondering the past? Or do we give the learner something to look forward to? Something new and exciting they can use right there on the job to reach their goals for the future. (Unless your job is digging in the past, of course.) At the same time, it's up to us designers to be creative and reuse— repurpose—what worked before by transforming it into something new. A reference that old-timers will recognize? You build instant secret connections. While new kids on the block will have no idea. And they don't care. If it's cool, it's cool. Good ideas don't have expiration dates.

Kid movies are filled with adult references that fly right over the kids' heads. And that is by design. Those are for the adults. Adults who can now feel that they're part of a secret club. The insiders. A joke that only the select understand. And even if you attempt to explain to your child that it was from a movie you saw when you were their age ...

The truth is, they don't care. So go and sample what works today. Look for new ways to integrate it with the future. People loved Pokémon. How about merging them with augmented reality? Dracula returned from old stories. Superheroes? Mix them, match them. You do not have to reinvent the wheel every time. Just be creative in how you spin it.

IRL CHALLENGES:

It's time for reflection! What was your original mojo number? Do the assessment again, and compare your mojo skills:

In real life, assess yourself on a 1 (no experience) to 10 (expert) scale on the six traits of the Magic Mojo Hexad. Add the six numbers together. This is your mojo power to start with:

1. **Critical Thinking** (From Order-taking to Problem-solving by Critical Thinking)
2. **CREAM** (From Page-turning to Mind-blowing by CReativity, Engagement, And Motivation)
3. **Adaptive Resilience** (From Passive Resistance to Adaptive Resilience by The Art of Bouncing Back)
4. **Human-Centered Design** (From Content to Context by Design

and Game Thinking)

5. **Social Impact** (From Silo to Sharing by Work-out-loud, Personal-brand, and Relationships)

6. **Myth Bunking** (From Learning Myths to the Real Workplace Thing by The Science of Learning, Artificial Intelligence, Evidence-Based Practicality, Knowledge-Skills-Attitude)

What have you learned through this journey? What would be one thing you want to share with others? How do you feel about the journey? Your thoughts are powering LI DOE's AI engine. Is she ready for the boss fight?

Chapter Nine

BOSS FIGHT
(FROM PAWN TO QUEEN???)

At noon, the Sun shines bright over the Castle. The Red King stands on the top of the Castle under the shade of an umbrella. He takes a deep breath, dips a chili pepper into his coffee. Down in the fields a White Bunny hops happily.

Red King: "Don't get too close. It's dark inside."

The White Bunny hops closer and closer to the Castle. From a dark corner, tens of Red Foxes charge out, and the chase is quick. The Red Fox tears the White Bunny apart, and drags the remains into the woods.

Red King: "There's nowhere we can hide."

The Cathedral's bells ring for noon. That moment a spinning LI DOE appears from the distant Scope Creep Creek. Then another LI

DOE shows up from thin air. Others pop up from underground. All of the spinning ghosts unite in one spinning dervish. Somewhat dizzy but determined, LI DOE proudly shows the Magic Mojo Hexad.

LI DOE: "Remember me? I have all six missing traits. I want to get promoted to Queen! Now!"

Red King: "LI DOE, I'm impressed. But I still can't promote you to Queen."

LI DOE: "I want to be promoted to Queen or I'll bring down this Castle!"

Red King: "Rook, my friend. Not Castle anymore. It's a Rook. But I can't promote you to Queen."

LI DOE: "Why not?"

That moment, the Scythe appears from above. This time LI DOE won't budge. LI DOE steps ahead. From the dark corners of the Castle Red Foxes snarl at LI DOE.

LI DOE: "You're not going to scare me! My magic mojo gives me full protection. I'll ask one more time: Look in my eye! Why can't you promote me to Queen?"

The Red King takes off his sunglasses to look straight into the eyes of LI DOE and snaps with his fingers. The Scythe moves into striking position.

Red King: "This is my kingdom come. Don't get too close!"

LI DOE steps forward. The Red Foxes growl. The Red King gestures, and the Scythe attacks. The Red Foxes charge for LI DOE. LI DOE raises the shield to reflect the Sun right into the eyes of the Red King. The Red King grabs his eyes in pain, and his sunglasses fall to the ground. Suddenly, the Red Foxes screech to a halt and run to the sunglasses. The Scythe changes direction and smashes into the ground, killing the Red Foxes.

LI DOE: "Oops."

The Red King regains his pose and control over the Scythe. The Scythe flies up in the air to strike again. LI DOE swiftly moves diagonally. The Scythe just misses LI DOE's legs, but it won't give up. LI DOE charges to the gate; the Scythe follows. Just when it would swing again, LI DOE slides sideways and does a 180-degree turn, using the shield again to reflect the Sun into the Red King's eyes. The Scythe smashes into the iron shield on the gate. It breaks into million pieces.

LI DOE: "I deserve to be Queen. I made history."

Red King: "You'll go down in history."

The Red King turns around and disappears inside the Castle. LI DOE walks to the gate and picks up the sunglasses: they're intact. Rabbit O'Reg appears with a massive lightning strike behind LI DOE.

LI DOE: "Oh, you? Not you again!"

Rabbit O'Reg: "You called me."

LI DOE: "Me? I didn't call anyone. Did you see? I just beat the Scythe! My shield protects me against anything."

LI DOE puts on the sunglasses and poses:

LI DOE: "Oppa. Gangnam Style!"

LI DOE produces a hilarious interpretation of the "Gangnam Style" moves that had ruled YouTube for five years. Nobody gets it. LI DOE hides the sunglasses and picks up the shield. It's a little dirty. She shakes it off.

LI DOE: "How about "Shake It Off"?"

Nobody is in a "swift" mood today.

Rabbit O'Reg: "Your shield didn't protect you."

LI DOE: "What do you mean? I collected all six traits. It's full protection."

Rabbit O'Reg: "It's an L&D shield. It's not for protection."

LI DOE: "Not for protection? Then what the heck is it for?"

Rabbit O'Reg: "For completely the opposite: exposure and reflection. It exposes you to danger. It pushes you out of your comfort zone. And you don't collect things; you gain them by experience and reflection."

LI DOE: "Wow. Then it will never help me get promoted to Queen?"

Rabbit O'Reg: "The Red King is right. He can't promote you to Queen."

LI DOE takes off the sunglasses.

LI DOE: "Why not?"

White Queen: "Because you are already Queen."

LI DOE: "Me? No. I'm a Pawn."

White Queen: "How do you know that?"

LI DOE: "How? Look! Can I run in any direction as far as I can see, like a Queen? Dancing? Disappearing in thin air? No. I'm a Pawn."

Rabbit O'Reg: "Look at your shield! Your shield has an upside-down Rook. An upside-down rook on the board is a Queen."

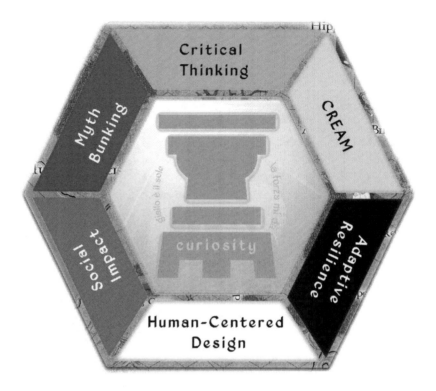

White Queen: "You've been a Queen all along."

LI DOE: "But … how come I couldn't do things like a Queen should be able to do?"

White Queen: "You can't do anything like a Queen because you need to think like a Queen before you can act like a Queen. Most of our limitations are self-imposed. It's all in our head. You can do everything a Queen should be able to do. It wasn't the shield that saved you from the Scythe. It was your swift moves. Your agility. Your adaptability. Your resilience. Determination. Creativity, motivation, and engagement.

Endgame

Eight Pawns join the team in front. Behind them two Rooks, Knights, Bishops, and the White Queen. The only piece missing from the chess line-up is the White King. As they look around, they're surrounded by hundreds of Red Foxes.

LI DOE: "Then why did you say I was a Pawn?"

White Queen: "I never said you were. I just said Pawns have limited thinking."

LI DOE: "But if I've been Queen all along, I could have gone home any time!"

White Queen: "Yes. You *can* go home any time. You only need to believe that there's an old world still out there where nothing changes. An old world that stays intact, as you like it, forever. But you are also one step away from breaking the spell here, and saving us from the Red King. It's your choice."

Silence ensues as lightning strikes right behind LI DOE. Rabbit O'Reg frowns at the sky. The Red Foxes howl.

Rabbit O'Reg: "Sorry. My bad."

LI DOE: "Fine. I'll break the spell and then I'll go home after."

Rabbit O'Reg: "Inside the Castle, there's the mirror to your old world. In a minute, the Red King will open the gate for you. If you break the spell, there's no going back. The Castle will be destroyed. You go home now or never."

White Queen: "You decide. If you have any questions left, this is the time to ask."

LI DOE: "Did you make the White King try this too? Is that how he ended up 'retired'?"

The White Queen sighs and looks at the Castle.

Rook: "Before the Red King built his Castle here, this was our favorite diner. We used to sit here, enjoying a cup of coffee before catching the train. Those were good times."

White Bishop: "Legend has it, flatmate, that the One will be remembered for centuries. Are you the One?"

LI DOE: "I am no One. I am no legend."

Rabbit O'Reg: "Some legends are told; some turn to dust or to gold. You are the One to break the spell and lead us to a new future. You're to turn the Red King's Castle to dust. You are also the One who can go back home as if nothing has happened, and turn this place to gold for the Red King. But, remember, you can't physically go anywhere unless you believe your mind is already there. You must believe that's what you want, and that's what you need."

As LI DOE picks up the shield, the gate opens. The Red King stands in the shade of the entrance, obviously looking for something on the ground. The Red Foxes slowly close in from all directions.

Red King: "Remember the good old days, beyond the looking class? The golden days of instructional design? Don't get too close. Forget this mess, the pain, the change, and return to your old world! Come inside and walk through the looking glass to return your own world."

LI DOE turns around to face the White Queen and the team.

LI DOE: "Sorry, folks!"

LI DOE walks toward the gate. As he almost makes it to the Red King, he suddenly stops. He lifts up his foot to spot something on the ground.

LI DOE stares at something on the ground. Then his attention focuses on the snarling Red Foxes surrounding the scene.

Red King: "What's that?"

LI DOE: "Nothing. Little things."

LI DOE continues to walk to the Red King. Two feet away from the gate she stops. She pulls out the sunglasses. Then she "accidentally" drops them.

LI DOE: "Oops! Don't get too close! This is where my demons hide."

The Red King slowly bends down to pick up the sunglasses. In the last moment LI DOE smashes them. As they crack into pieces, the Red Foxes howl and go into full attack. The Red King swings at LI DOE, but she swiftly moves out of the way. The Red King blows up in the air. The Red Foxes fly up to the sky and turn into fireworks. The Castle shakes.

Bang! Dust covers everything.

LI DOE: "Oops."

The Castle collapses with a bright explosion. The Cathedral bell rings again, and rain starts falling hard on the dust. As the dust settles in the pouring rain, the silhouette of a small diner is revealed. A tall man wearing a white apron steps out with fresh-brewed divine-smelling coffee.

Tom: "Oh, this rain! Hello, everyone! C'mon in! Welcome to Tom's Diner!"

Tom raises his mug to the White Queen. LI DOE catches a moment between them.

LI DOE: "Hey, you never answered my question."

White Queen: "About the White King? He's happily retired from dealing with the *big things* of the WORL&D. But what changed your mind about going back to you world?"

LI DOE: "*Little things* of the WORL&D."

IRL CHALLENGES:

1. Stop and reflect for 10 minutes:

What are 5 "little things" you would absolutely miss if they disappeared from your life?

Chapter Ten

TOM'S DINER

LI DOE is dipping a red chili pepper into his coffee. Across the table Rabbit O'Reg sucks on his empty pipe. The place is cozy and filled with happy patrons. LI DOE points at the shield with all six traits collected.

LI DOE: "So, now that I got stuck here, what shall I do with this? I'm finished."

Rabbit O'Reg: "Like a book, it's never finished. You just stop writing. You are never finished. You just stop learning."

LI DOE: "So, what's next? What am I going to do here with my future?"

Rabbit O'Reg: "The six traits you've collected will expose you to the change that's coming. Are these the only ones you'll need? No. But it's a good start. Congrats! You've completed Level 1. Your AI features are now activated for Level 2."

LI DOE: "What AI features?"

Rabbit O'Reg: "You'll find it out in the future, around Appendix A."

MENTAL TRAVEL: The Future (Where We Learn About AI)

In *Learning in the Age of Immediacy,* Brandon Carson walks us through five disruptive technologies that are changing the WORL&D. Today, it might seem still like science fiction to work alongside robots powered by artificial intelligence.

At the same time, I can remember some of my initial doubts in the last two decades:

- Pentium motherboard? For personal use? Ridiculous.

- Who would want to carry a giant piece of equipment as a mobile phone?
- Why would anyone want to be online all the time?
- Ordering books online is fine, but I would never order groceries.

Many of these initial resistance thoughts were formed based on the experience we had with products at that point of time. Early products are exciting, but they suck. The first cell phone? It was like carrying a car battery in your bag. Lessons learned? Don't judge based on the MVP (minimum viable product) but, rather, on the vision behind it. The vision is what we, as L&D, should be focusing on. It's about where the puck goes, not where it is, you know.

What's our place in the future? Are automation and AI really going to free us up from tedious, error-prone tasks? And with that free time, will we be able to focus on more innovative work? (Weren't computers promising the same thing, to automate a lot of tedious tasks, so we could have more freedom? Have they?) In the last fifteen years, we introduced "smart" things in technology. Smart chips, smart phones, and smart houses appeared. In the next ten years or so, we might see "AI-powered" taking over. Of course, marketing needs to come up with a way to distinguish between the old smart and the new smart. Maybe the new tech will be more intelligent than just smart?

Will the coming change in technology affect L&D? No. It's affecting L&D now. How people live and work are being affected as we speak. Learning is no longer a controlled substance exposure happening only under L&D supervision in an LMS lab. Content is everywhere. Lifelong learning happens with or without L&D.

One of the biggest change that is happening to the WORL&D today is that learning itself is becoming part of the modern workplace surviving skills for individuals. Learning is no longer the private sandbox that L&D owns. We're sharing the sandbox with everyone else. The gates are open 24/7. We're not writing the rules of engagement anymore like in the old days. And so, our challenge will be to become much more nimble, much more context-focused, and move away from the "approved content for all" approach. As individuals at the modern workplace take responsibility for their own learning, stakeholders and SMEs will change their needs for support. And L&D needs to be ready for that. There will be a time when we laugh that instead of a checklist, delivered at the point of need, we took five weeks to build a course that nobody found effective. The era of floppy disc is over.

FINAL MENTAL TRAVEL: Machine Learning, 1993 (Where I Build Machine Learning on a Floppy Disc)

Machine learning isn't new. In 1993, I approached a professor about my thesis (nothing too critical, just wondering what should it be about). I wanted to do something different. He gave me an article (this was pre-internet). It was about how to build artificial neural networks using machine learning. It was in English! I loved the challenge. What could possibly go wrong?

I almost didn't graduate. Imagine an artificial neural network as layers of connected neurons. One layer receives some kind of input, and the other creates the output. In between? Multitudes of hidden layers. My neural network was supposed to learn how to add two numbers together. Machine learning relies on data. Lots of data. You show data to the network—in my case, two numbers—and the network comes up with an output. Out of the box, it's dumb as a gompie. Next, you show what the output should be. The network compares the two results and adjusts itself. This is where the magic happens. It runs an algorithm to adjust every single connection. Then it starts again: two input data creating an output, comparing it with the actual result, adjustment. This happens over and over and over. Slowly, the network learns the pattern.

I was watching one number for weeks on my monitor. It was the number representing how "confident" the network was in the learning process. The neural network didn't calculate the correct number, it calculated an outcome, and told me how confident it was that the outcome was the correct result. In order to graduate, that "error" had to be low enough that I could defend my thesis. When I forced the network to learn faster (doing big adjustments in a cycle), it blew up. When I let it run with too small of adjustments, it didn't improve fast enough.

That was in 1993. I saved my neural network on a floppy disk. Today, powerful machines in the cloud have the capacity to power real AI-driven applications. We've come a long way from the floppy disk. With that, needs in demand are changing as well. Google "learning jobs"! You'll find lots of machine learning engineer positions open. Learning is not about content building anymore.

One skill, I predict, will remain in demand: the ability to ask the right questions. Everyone has its own Red King out there, hiding in the borders of your comfort zone. Use your shield! Step out! Expose yourself! Reflect! Your curiosity will be your GPS! Because curiosity is like a hole: the more the Red Kings of the WORL&D try to take from it, the bigger and deeper it gets. Be curious! Experiment! See something? Share something! Engage others! Engage your audience! You're not alone! Thanks for reading this. Now, let's join our forces in the fight against the Red Kings of the WORL&D! Engage the WORL&D!

I hope my "meme-oir" served you well! By the end of this module you've consumed the mental tapas–style entree, with freshly dug ingredients such as memories turned a-ha moments harvested in the field of learning and development, topped with a pinch of whimsicality spice, a dash of humor, and sprinkles of memes. You've enjoyed it served chilled for L&D, especially if you're an instructional designer. You've paired it with your favorite glass of beverage, relaxed, continued to breathe, and now, you're ready to get out there and engage the WORL&D! Cheers!

Closing Time

Last call in Tom's Diner. Rabbit O'Reg opens up the paper, there's an article about an actor who died, so he flips to the horoscopes. Meanwhile, he casually throws out the question to LI DOE.

Rabbit O'Reg: "So, what changed your mind after all?"

Rabbit O'Reg turns to the funnies section.

Tom: "Last call!"

Rabbit O'Reg: "What was on the ground. Is that what changed your mind?"

LI DOE: "No. What wasn't on the ground. Little thing..."

Their thoughts are interrupted by the White Queen's ominous expression. She's outside in the rain, her hair is wet but she's more concerned about the reflection she sees in the window. Tom freezes behind the counter while pouring coffee. LI DOE's Future-Gazing Mixed-Reality Goggles clearly show the consequences if they do not act ASAP. Time for change.

Welcome to Level 2.

LI DOE's AI Framework

APPENDIX A

LI DOE'S AI TRAITS AND FEATURES

Technical specification document on the Last ID On Earth (LI DOE), version 1.71.

LI DOE's AI Feature Framework of Traits

Trait #1: Critical Thinking

"Am I asking the right questions?" is one of the most powerful questions to ask. Simply thinking about your thinking, whether you're even asking questions, is critical in the process of moving from order-taker to problem-solver. While this question triggers self-reflection most of the time, you can also use it to tackle the unknowns. For example, you can ask this question at the end of a needs analysis meeting: "Are we asking the right questions? What other questions should we be asking?"

The **BS 360 Buzzword Detection Nose** helps you identify "trends" in the field. These are mostly new and shiny objects to chase. They may not be useful in learning, but in the early days, they're sold as a cure-for-all. Why is that? Vendors and consultants who create products (platform, applications, frameworks, etc.) first in market have the initial financial advantage. They must sell the solution fast, before others catch up and competition takes place. If I invested a lot in a "solution" (it might be a really great solution for some problems), I want to sell this solution to every problem remotely related to the target. This is how you make money. If you believe your solution cures the color gray, there's fifty shades you might target. And who knows, it might be a workaround for those who are suffering from dark blue as well.

I've seen in many an organization (especially if IT is involved) that once a "solution" is purchased, that solution is forced on various problems it was never intended to address. Call this the "Rainbow Solution."

Whether it's an authoring tool, a learning management system, or an engagement platform, beware the rainbow effect. For example, "mobile first" doesn't mean upload as many videos as you can to your new video platform, so you can claim you're doing mobile. Mobile first doesn't mean strategy next. A platform should not drive a solution. Design the solution first, then find the technology to support it.

Trait #2: CREAM

Who doesn't like cream? Whether ice, whipped, or heavy, cream makes everything fun and exciting. So do **CReativity, Engagement And Motivation**. One of HR's biggest challenges in today's world is "talent engagement." Losing top talents is expensive. It's interesting to look back at the predictions for 2017 in Josh Bersin's "HR Technology Disruptions for 2017: Nine Trends Reinventing the HR Software Market."[43]

Fast forward to 2017, the real deal: "The corporate L&D market is undergoing one of its most disruptive times in the last 15 years.[...] While all of this has been going on, L&D has been trying to reinvent itself and is now adopting design thinking, starting to build apps, and realizing that it has to become video producers, not just instructional designers. In many ways, I believe the L&D profession is more exciting and fun now than it has been for a decade..."[44]

This is an exciting time to enter the field of learning! Stop focusing on content. The value of L&D is not in the course content, it's in the experience. It's invisible in people's minds. It's about making people's lives easier. In fact, the best motivation you can offer is staying out of people's lives with unnecessary courses! And that's a worthy cause!

Creativity brings freshness to workplace learning. Creativity leads to meaningful challenges, which in return produces engagement. Engagement doesn't start with boring content topped with gamification or chunked in microlearnings. Constant feedback loops allow humans to adjust and adapt to change, nudge by nudge. Providing them with a vision to strive for, instead of turn-by-turn instructions, can transfer engagement into motivation and, in the long run, maybe inspiration. You

---

43   https://www2.deloitte.com/content/dam/Deloitte/us/Documents/human-capital/us-hc-disruptions.pdf .

44   https://www2.deloitte.com/content/dam/Deloitte/at/Documents/about-deloitte/predictions-for-2017-final.pdf

can't start this process midway and just build a "workplace engagement" program. Instructional designers have to start to work closely with business; they have to step out of the learning bubble. The more you know about your audience, the more empathy you gain, which leads to more realistic, better experiences. The best way to do that is through work. Once a month, just for a day, try to do someone else's work.

The **xTreme Empathy Storyteller** feature allows you to deliver messages, even learning, through stories that move the audience, rather than spitting out dry facts. The **Engagement Adventure Pack** is a lightweight bag of tools and tricks you can mobilize anywhere. You're not confined to a desk (or 9 to 5 work hours) anymore. The **Hands-On Problem-Solver** feature powers you to take all the wonderful theory that you know about learning and laser-focus-apply them to solve real problems in a context, not in an LMS. In today's world, performance is so intertwined with tools, applications, people, and processes that learning must be seamlessly woven into problem-solving. You must go through the looking class!

Trait #3: Adaptive Resilience

As we said before, L&D is going through the biggest disruption of standard operation in fifteen years. There's going to be a lot of change (and therefore a lot of adapting!). I'm sure we all know it's not going to be a straight line to success. How to stay relevant in the midst of change? What skills and knowledge should you focus on? What happens when you fail? It's not an if, it's a when. Many whens, actually. What's good about the time of disruption is that failure is tolerated, if not encouraged. Fail soon and fail often goes the saying in the start-up world. With that, what you need is the ability to bounce back. Resilience is the art of bouncing back. **Resilience** is not just standing up again. It's not like a computer system restoration to a safe point yesterday if something goes wrong today. That's not going to help with the change. You must learn from the experience, unlearn the old ways, adapt, and try again. Without adapting, you will run into the same results over and over again.

The **Resilience Boots on the Ground** will help you stabilize yourself for small shakes. They won't stop you from falling, but every time you land on the ground, they learn something new (even if you don't). They adapt to the ground. Think of them as the AI of bottom soles. The **Future-Gazing Mixed-Reality Goggles** are more than just cool glasses. They are looking ahead to predict changes to come. With fore-seeing what's ahead, you have more time to adapt and innovate to avoid a fall. Why mixed reality? In the near future, the three worlds (real, augmented, and virtual) might live as one. Just like in John Lennon's song about AI: "I hope some day you'll join us. And the world will be as one." (Songs and lyrics will often interfere with my storytelling, as you might have noticed.)

Trait #4: Human-Centered Design

As L&D moves toward a problem-solver role, we must master a new approach: We need to focus on humans, not "learners." In the modern workplace, there are no learners. There are humans who have thousands of things going on in their lives. We must solve challenges before they are declared a "training problem." So often I see training as the suggested solution problems that stem from poor for design in the first place (such as badly designed applications). **Design Thinking** helps us find better solutions, centered around the actual users rather than on someone in the IT Department who never has to use the application. In the design process, we must apply best practices of **UI** (user interface) and **UX** (user experience). Without oversimplifying the two different concepts, imagine reading a book. The pages, the fonts, the layout, even the paragraphs are all part of the UI for you, the reader. But that's not why you want to read more from the author. The experience (which includes the UI) of reading a great book is the UX. As you know, the same book with the same UI might not be everyone's favorite book. That's why UX is much more about humans and their needs/desires/motivations than about technology. As the heart of Design Thinking is about the exploration of the human nature, UX and Design Thinking often synch up very well. Along with Design Thinking, engagement and motivation might be supported by **Game Thinking**. Game Thinking isn't about building games or gamification. It's a systematic approach to problem-solving, where engagement and motivation play a key role. You might end up with a game or you may end up with gamification; you might even end up with something in between, as simple as gameful design. Both Design Thinking and Game Thinking are centered around humans, hence the title "Human-Centered Design."

Trait #5: Social Impact

One mistake we committed in the early 2000s was letting technology take over and dominate the wonders of eLearning. The beauty of electronic delivery and learning management systems tracking made us forget why we built the whole thing in the first place. The man versus machine in an LMS bubble with enforced templates and logos (yes, they are branded, though!!) turned eLearning into a curse word. I want to give credit to all who didn't fall into the trap and continued the effort of turning eLearning into an engaging, interactive learning experience—what it should have been in the first place! Working is team play! Why do we force "learning" into a singles torture tournament in the LMS? Workplace learning should focus on humans, not technology and trends that look good on the annual performance goals for those who select and buy them but never use them. (Okay, maybe I'm exaggerating here and you never had to figure out how to exclude senior leadership from those nasty automatic LMS emails that remind them to take courses.) I often see this conversation taking place on LinkedIn: "How do you promote your learning assets?" The answer could be as simple as: "By making them worthwhile to talk about." There's nothing better than overhearing people discussing your "learning asset" around the proverbial watercooler.

Wrinkle-Free Personal Brand, you might say, is an optional thing. Not everyone is a celebrity and influencer. I believe everyone is an influencer, but some people just choose not to influence. I might be wrong, but your personal brand (what people think and say about you when you leave the room) can make or mark your best effort when working with stakeholders. If you don't have credibility, your questions will project instability, insecurity, and, more likely, you will revert back to order-taking. If your personal brand is about expertise, trust, and reliability, you'll have a much easier time asking the hard questions that need to be asked. Personal brand is both offline and online. Who do you follow? Who do they follow? How do you know if you should know about something? Build a personal learning network (PLN) and ask them questions, share ideas you're working on. Don't work in the SILO! It's exhausting to be on your own.

That's why you need the **Social Collab Halo**. Most people are naturally nice and ready to help. But you need to build that relationship. And one more thing: it's okay to say you don't know the answer and you need help. If you know all the answers all the time, it's time to grow.

Trait #6: Myth Bunking

Myth bunking is the debunking process for L&D. It's the process of differentiating between urban legends and research-based reality. This area includes the science of learning, how the brain (supposedly) works, evidence-based methods, and future trends. The **Rolled-Up Sleeves Attitude** represents your ability and willingness to do your homework on research data. Find the source for data you're sharing. If you see an even number on a colorful infographic with no sources, be skeptical. Ask! A lot of myths out there just won't die because people with good intentions keep sharing them.

One of the challenges learning professionals face is that scientific studies often end with limitations. Those limitations and further questions are IMPORTANT! You can't cherry pick facts from a study to fit your beliefs, while ignoring facts you don't like. Just like dealing with fake news, it's a good idea to check before you disseminate.

The **Adaptive Leather Flying Hat** has built-in artificial intelligence. Think of an extension of your natural intelligence. It's lightweight, ready for any adventure, and protects your head against noise. There's a lot of noise happening in the learning space, and when you're flying a thousand miles per hour, the change of winds can be deafening. The built-in communication equipment allows you to tune in to any channel you need, and one of those channels is actually you. Listening to your own thoughts might be strange at first. But let me tell you something I learned while reading over eighty books as preparation to write my own: somehow, somewhere, there was one notion that came up in almost all of them: mindfulness. Mindfulness is the basic human ability to be fully present, aware of where you are, what you're doing, and not overwhelmed by the WORL&D around you.

The **Practicality Hipster Toolkit (PHT)** has nothing to do with being hip,. It's about being practical, flexible, and fast. If you're lucky enough to work in a place where pure instructional design principles rule the land, this book is not for you. If you're swimming against the tides of tight resources, deadlines, and budgets, while quality cannot be compromised, where you need to apply the vast knowledge about learning but you must be quick, flexible, and practical, you'll find value in the examples. Some call it compromising; some call it prioritizing; some just say scrappy.

Underlying Engine Fuel: Curiosity

Intellectual curiosity is the driving fuel of your creativity and innovation engine. Curiosity isn't a scheduled event, it's a never-ending squelch of knowledge thirst. Curiosity forces you to see the WORL&D from different angles. Some people just want to know how to do things to master a process. Curious people want to know the whys (and why nots!). Creativity is seeing connections, patterns, before anyone else does. Innovation is executing on the vision to make an impact. Neither would exist without curiosity. Thoughts of curiosity often include "why" and "what if" in the context of observing the WORL&D. You can challenge yourself, for example, by looking at various signs wherever you travel, asking: "Why is that sign there?" One of my favorite examples is "No spitting in the waiting room!" Hmm…

226

APPENDIX B

STUFF TO READ

Over a year, I've been reading excellent books from bright minds that helped me on the journey of writing my own. I wanted to share this list with you:

How Learning Works: Seven Research-Based Principles for Smart Teaching	Ambrose, Susan A.
Self-Publishing: Cover Design, Hardcover Book Cover Creation For Lulu, How To Create Your Cover For CreateSpace (Do It Yourself Guide, For Beginners)	Baird, Chris A.
Blindspot: Hidden Biases of Good People	Banaji, Mahzarin R.
Ebook: Design Thinking (Innovation Trends Series)	BBVA Innovation Center
The Accidental Instructional Designer: Learning Design for the Digital Age	Bean, Carolyn
Expanding the Self: The Intelligent Complex Adaptive Learning System: A New Theory of Adult Learning (The Knowledge Series)	Bennet, David
How to Talk about Videogames (Electronic Mediations)	Bogost, Ian
Play to Learn: Everything You Need to Know About Designing Effective Learning Games	Boller, Sharon

228

About the Author

Zsolt Olah is a digital learning strategist, speaker, leader, and doer with 20+ years of experience in driving performance through learning. Zsolt is a frequent speaker at learning conferences (ATD TK, ATD ICE, DevLearn) and game thinking workshops. His in-depth knowledge of technology and instructional design, coupled with creativity and innovative thinking, has been the driving force behind successful learning and performance solutions for various happy clients.

Zsolt is happy to connect with everyone on social media who wants to get engaged in shaping the "now of learning," instead of talking about the future of learning. Engage the WORL&D!

Made in the USA
Lexington, KY
12 January 2019